John and Pat Underwood

walk & eat NICE

CONTENTS

This pocket guide is designed for short break walking holidays based on Nice, using public transport (or a car, if you prefer). The city is easily and inexpensively reached by several budget airlines, and the climate makes for brilliant walking and excursions all year round.

Hop on a plane for a long weekend or a week. You have in your hand enough walks, excursions, restaurants and recipes to last almost two weeks — so you can pick and choose the most appealing. The highlights at a glance:

- 12 varied day walks, each with topographical map
- 2 fairly long excursions — one by train, one by bus, with walks from each
- recommended restaurants and hotels
- recipes to make at your self-catering base or back home
- special section with hints on wheat-, gluten- and dairy-free eating and cooking in the south of France

INTRO

THE WALKS

The walks range from flat coastal rambles a 15-minute bus ride from the city to 'balcony' routes high above the famed Riviera and mountain circuits. The book is specifically designed for visitors using public transport. If you've only a long weekend, you may not want to spend time filling in forms to hire a car. Of course, if you *do* want to hire a car, you will have many more options in the hinterland. Our wider-ranging book, *Landscapes of Eastern Provence* (see www.sunflowerbooks.co.uk), would take you from the Italian border to the Rhône via 11 car tours and 36 walks.

But rest assured that you do not need your own wheels to cut a large swathe through the 'Pays niçois'. All the walks in this book are easily reached by bus or train, and getting to the walks is half the fun. Sightsee while someone else does the driving. It's amazing how much ground you can cover in just a week.

THE EXCURSIONS

Two long trips are outlined. First is the wonderful rail journey on the 'Train des Pignes', a narrow-gauge railway built between 1890 and 1912. It begins right in the city centre, running on 'tram' lines, then spans 150km on its journey into the mountains. The scenery is awe-inspiring. The train is an ideal way to reach walks out of town.

The second excursion is by local bus up the Var Valley and then via the red-rock Cians Gorges, up to ski resort country, where you can take an idyllic circular walk.

THE RESTAURANTS

There are restaurants and hotels at the start or end of many of the walks, most of which we mention. But many of them close out of season — just when the walking is at its best! Unless we know that a restaurant will welcome you all year round, we suggest that you return to Nice for dinner — perhaps making a local recipe yourself. *No restaurant has paid, in cash or in kind, to be included in this guide.*

Several of our recommended restaurants are at hotels where you might like to spend the night, especially if you want to have dinner there and there is no late public transport back to base.

THE RECIPES

Most of our recommended restaurants were happy to share with us the *ingredients* used in their recipes, but the actual preparation remains their 'secret' (in truth, they are simply not written down, but just passed on from cook to cook over the years). So you can rest assured that we have cooked *all* of these recipes ourselves, to make sure they 'work'!

What we cannot guarantee, of course, is that they will taste as good back home as they did in France! So many factors come into play to make food taste better when you are on holiday — from the intangibles (the atmosphere and the sense of relaxation after a day's good walking) to the tangibles (hardness of the water, quality of the fresh market produce you can seek out when not pressed for time). So if you are in self-catering, why not try some of these recipes while you're in Nice?

We've made most of these dishes on the simple kind of cooker usually found in self-catering (two rings and a decent oven) — or on a barbecue. Many of them are casserole-style, not only easily managed with limited cooking facilities, *but* also virtually impossible to overcook, and there is hardly any washing-up! What's more, they always taste better when reheated after a few days. And good news for anyone suffering food intolerances: all of the recipes can be **gluten- and dairy-free** (see page 138).

PLANNING YOUR VISIT

When to go

The simple answer is — anytime outside mid-June to mid-September, when it's usually swelteringly hot, crowded to overflowing, and prices are at their highest. (Moreover, areas prone to forest fires — like the Esterel, see Walk 5 — may be closed to visitors from mid-July until mid-September.)

New Year's Day lunch on the beach at Nice

We walk from Nice in all other months. Naturally late September and October are ideal for the mild temperatures and the autumnal colours in the hinterland. One has to take a chance with autumnal rains in October and November, but you can still expect temperatures in the 60s (17-20°C).

We often go at Christmas/New Year, to enjoy the festivities

and the clear winter skies. If you think it may be too cold, remember that New Year's Day lunch on the beach is a long-standing tradition in Nice!

February ushers in carnival, mimosa festivals, and more good walking — it's virtually spring. Plan on some rainy days in March and April, but rainy spells don't usually last very long. And at least when it rains in Nice, there's plenty to do indoors (apart from trying new recipes).

May and early June, with wild flowers galore, are simply glorious, as you would expect.

Where to stay

Of course there is a wide choice of hotels of all grades all along the coastal strip from Cannes to Menton. But the *best* public transport base is Nice centre.

Rather than an hotel, consider staying in private accommodation or one of the apart-hotels in the city. One chain we have used is the Citadines (www.citadines.com); another is Séjours du Sud (www.sejoursdusud.com), where we cooked most of our recipes at the apart-hotel Nice Fleurs.

To find an apartment, just search 'apartments in Nice' on the web; Google, for instance, throws up hundreds of sites, including many privately-owned second homes.

What to take

Remembering that this is to be a carefree week or weekend, pack simply! You don't have to 'dress' for dinner in Nice, no matter how elegant the restaurant.

We manage with a rucksack each, by wearing our walking boots on the flight. Apart-hotels have inexpensive laundry facilities (and there are also many laundries and launderettes in the city), so you needn't take a lot of clothing either.

The big wheel is a feature of festival time in Nice

No special equipment is needed for any of the walks, but proper **walking boots** are preferable to any other footwear. Most walks in the Nice hinterland cross very stony terrain at some stage, and good ankle support is essential. In wet weather you will also be glad of the waterproofing. A **sunhat** and high-protection **suncream** are equally important; there is a real risk of sunstroke on some walks (especially in May/June). Each member of the party should carry a small rucksack, so that the chore of lugging the essentials is shared. *All year round* it is advisable to carry a first-aid kit, whistle, torch, spare socks and bootlaces, and some warm clothing (the *mistral* can blow up suddenly, with temperatures dropping up to 10°C/20°F!). A long-sleeved shirt and long trousers should be worn or carried, for sun protection and for making your way through the prickly plants of the *maquis*. Depending on the season, you may also need a windproof, lightweight rainwear, woollies and gloves. Optional items include swimwear, a Swiss Army knife (but *don't* pack this in hand luggage, or it will be confiscated), and insect repellent. Mineral water is sold almost everywhere in plastic half-litre bottles (which you can then refill from the tap); ***it is imperative that each walker carries at least a half-litre of water — a full litre or more in hot weather.***

Planning your walks

The walks are specifically designed for access by the excellent **local transport** network ... so that you can enjoy a bottle of wine with lunch! But if you *do* want to hire a **car**, and the route is linear, you can usually leave your car at the end of the walk and take a bus to the start.

The walks have been **graded** for the deskbound person who nevertheless keeps reasonably fit. Our timings average 4km per hour on the flat, plus 20 minutes for every 100m/300ft of ascent. None of the walks ascends more than about 500m/1650ft, although there are one or two steep descents. *Do* check your timings against ours on a short walk before tackling one of the longer hikes. Remember that these are *neat walking times;* increase the overall time by *at least* 50 percent, to allow for any breaks and nature-watching.

Safety depends in great part on *knowing what to expect and being properly equipped.* For this reason we urge you to read through the *whole* walk description at your leisure *before* setting out, so that you have a mental picture of each stage of the route and the landmarks. On *most* of our walks you will encounter other people — an advantage if you get into difficulty. Nevertheless, we advise you **never** to walk alone.

The **maps** in this book, adapted from the latest IGN 1:25,000 maps, have been reproduced at a scale of 1:35,000 or larger. The relevant map numbers, should you wish to go further afield, are shown in the 'logistics' panel facing each walk introduction. All the latest IGN maps (the 'Top 25' Series) show many local and long-distance walks.

Of the dozens of reasons why walking from Nice is such a joy, a particularly strong point is the superb **waymarking** and **signposting** carried out by the governing bodies of the Alpes Maritimes and Alpes de Haute Provence.

Basically you will encounter two types of waymarked route:

PR (Petite Randonnée) or 'short walk' routes, waymarked in yellow and usually signposted;

GR (Grande Randonnée) or 'long-distance' routes, waymarked in red and white, but not generally signposted.

At the top of each walk we mention the waymarking colours *at time of writing*. Do, however, note these waymarking features, common to both PR and GR routes:

— A *flash* (stripe of paint) or *dot* (stipple of paint) indicates 'Route continues this way'. (The GR uses *two separate* flashes, red and white, and this must *never* be confused with a red flash on a white paint background, which is forestry marking, *not* route marking.)

— A right- or left-angled flash (or an arrow) means 'Change of direction'.

— An X means 'Wrong way'.

Verifying timetables in advance

While transport details are given in the 'logistics' panel at the start of each walk, remember that these timetables were *correct at time of writing*. The *very best* way to verify departures and returns is at the information desk at the relevant stations after you arrive. But if you want to plan some walks in advance, you can verify most timetables online before you travel.

Trains are operated by TER (Transports Express Régional), part of the SNCF (Société Nationale des Chemins de Fer). Their web site is **www.ter-sncf.com**. (You may spot a British flag, but in our experience the English version doesn't work reliably). On getting the site up, a map appears. Below is an example, based on Walk 5.

- click on 'Provence-Alpes-Côte d'Azur'
- at 'Mon point de départ' type in Nice
- at 'Mon point d'arrivée' type in Théoule-sur-Mer
- at box 'Date de mon trajet' fill in a theoretical day for the week you will visit and the earliest time you want to catch a train
- at box 'Je souhaite', leave 'Partir vers'
- at box 'Mes préférences' leave default (as fast as possible)
- then click 'Lancer la recherche'

Now about three departure times will come up to view; arrival times and total journey times are also shown. To see *earlier* times, click below on 'Horaires précédents'; to see *later* times, click on 'Horaires suivants'.

- now click on 'Trajet retour'; the site automatically shows you three departures from Théoule to Nice

Golden-hued 18th-century façades grace Old Nice; above: old town hall

Timetables for the delightful, privately-owned **Train de Pignes**, operated by the Chemins de Fer de Provence (Excursion 1, Walks 9 and 10), *cannot* be accessed at ter-sncf. To see their timetables, go to **www.trainprovence.com**, then click on 'Nice > Digne-les-Bains', then on 'Horaires', where you can download a PDF.

Intercity buses are operated by TAM (Transports Alpes-Maritimes); their web site is at **www.cg06.fr/transport/transports-tam.html**. It is very easy to use. Under 'Lignes et horaires', just scroll down to the bus line you want (shown in the 'Logistics' panel with each walk.

Nice bus station is very well organised

While this method works for *most* buses you will want, the TAM network is comprised of several individual operators, some of whom haven't any web sites of their own and haven't posted their times on the TAM site. For example, at the time of writing there was no timetable on the web for Bus 902 from Menton to Ste-Agnès (Walk 7), although the return bus 903 from Castellar *is* shown! Hopefully the site links will improve in future, but at present the only way to verify our departure times for this bus is at the bus station in Menton.

Note also that you can telephone the bus stations direct, and *usually* contact an English-speaking person: Nice bus station *(gare routière):* ✆ 04 93 85 61 81; Menton bus station *(gare routière):* ✆ 04 93 35 93 60.

City buses are operated by Ligne d'Azur (**www.lignedazur.com**). Their site is very easy to use and can be accessed in English. Just select the specific destination you want and download the pdf file.

ON ARRIVAL

City bus pass

Your first stop, still at the airport, should be the 'bus station' (the left-hand exit from the terminal). Buy a suitable **Ligne d'Azur pass**; there are several on offer, from a 1-day pass to a 'multi+' which gives 17 trips and can be used by more than one person. You'll be amazed how far your pass will take you!

Ask for **'le plan'** — a map of their routes, which is indispensable. You can also download this map from their web site (shown opposite) in advance; click on 'Maps'.

Then just take one of the frequent city buses from the airport into town. Each time you board a bus, you must *validate* the ticket by inserting it (with the arrow pointing down) into the machine behind the driver.

The main **Ligne d'Azur office** is at 10 Avenue Félix Faure, in the Grand Hotel Aston (opposite 5 on the plan). It is open 07.15-17.00 Mon-Fri, 07.15-16.00 Sat (✆ 04 93 13 53 13). They stock 'le plan' and printed timetables for all the city bus routes in this book. And they offer the widest variety of passes.

Tourist information

The **tourist office** (1 on the plan), on the Promenade des Anglais near the famous Hotel Negresco (22), could be one of your first ports of call, to find out what's on during your visit and to pick up a **city plan**. Very close by is the Caffé Promenade (28; see page 103) and, five blocks west, the Café Pinocchio (27; see caption on page 16)

We're becoming quite the experts on hot chocolate. We almost always have one by 11am — or earlier, if there's a bus to catch.
Coffee after dinner keeps us awake, and we don't like decaf, so sometimes we have a hot chocolate at Le Pot d'Etain (see page 56). Michèle uses a cocoa from Maxim's (the famous Paris restaurant) — and lovely it is, too — especially with a brandy. Dark chocolate and brandy is a very happy combination.
Another place for a delicious morning chocolate is the Caffé Promenade (see page 103).
But the utter *nirvana* for those who like really rich chocolate is the Café Pinocchio on the corner of Gambetta and the Promenade des Anglais (27 on the plan). They sell an Italian cocoa called Eraclea Antica, in cups provided by the manufacturer. This is certainly the best hot chocolate ever — and we drink it *without* milk!

Shopping for self-catering

Even if you are foregoing the luxury of staying in someone's beautifully equipped 'second home' in Nice (see 'Where to stay', page 8), aparthotels should have good-quality kitchenettes with small fridges, two-ring electric burners and, more importantly, quite a good-sized oven. There is ample crockery, cutlery and cooking utensils, but you may want to pick up a few extra things, like a vegetable peeler and whisk.

Although more exotic shopping trips will come later, make your first port of call the nearest **supermarket,** to stock up on essentials. The two main supermarket chains in Nice are the Casino and the Intermarché. We blitz the nearest Casino on arrival, and stock up on staples.

But supermarkets also

Supermarket shopping list reminder
washing-up liquid or dishwasher tablets
paper towels
aluminium foil
soap
tissues/toilet paper
scouring pads
salt & pepper
mineral water
milk/cream*
coffee/tea/drinking chocolate
butter*
sugar
bread*
juice
wine/beer/cider
olive oil & vinegar
eggs
tomato purée
rice
mayonnaise/mustard
torch batteries?
vegetable peeler?
whisk?

*see also panel on page 137 for gf, df supermarket products

have delicatessens, butchers and fishmongers, and this is an easy option if you're shopping in the afternoon or on a Sunday, when the local markets aren't usually open.

Markets

Once the staples are in the cupboard, the real shopping fun can begin. Our nearest **market** is the **Marché da la Buffa** (29 on the plan). It's open from 07.00 to 13.00 every day and has a great many stalls (not *all* are open *every day*).

It's best to just spend an hour looking round at first, to size up the varied produce, then go back to where you want

Seafood on display at the Marché de la Buffa

An artist's palette of spices on Rue Pairolière — everything from anise to ... rosebuds with black peppercorns. Below: some shops sell nothing but olives — and Nice's own virgin olive oil.

to buy. One stall sells nothing but fresh herbs. There are delicatessens, butchers, poulterers, fishmongers, a huge variety of fruit and veg purveyors, and cheese stands galore. If you get weary, there's a bar or two as well...

But undoubtedly *the* most pleasant place to shop — not only for food, but for all kinds of craftwork, is in **Old Nice**, south of Place Garibaldi (7 on the plan). Walk south out of Garibaldi on the wide Boulevard Jean Jaurès, then take the second left turn into **Rue Pairolière**. This is the main shopping street of the old town, an assault on all the senses! Whole shops are devoted to nothing but dried herbs and spices — or olives — or bread — or soap. Not far along you pass René Socca (see page 26; 30 on the plan).

If you've come early enough and aren't ready for lunch, you might want to continue along Rue François and then fork left on Rue Benoit Bunico. Keep straight on, and you will come to the vibrant **Cours Saleya** (8), where there's a food and flower market every morning (except Mondays, when the whole area is given over to the famous antiques market).

At Christmas (and some other festivals) many 'one-man bands' set out stalls at Place Massena. This sausage- and cheese-maker from the Pyrenees is our favourite (and we haven't even tried the 'Viagra' sausage yet!).

Dipping your toes into a Cote d'Azur walking holiday couldn't be easier – you can start in the city of Nice, by strolling round three mini-mountains with beautiful woodlands and gardens, ancient remains and breathtaking views.

1 WALK
on the rooftops of nice

Distance: about 8km/5mi; 3h

Grade: Quite easy, with little ascent; descents (mostly on steps) of about 300m/1000ft overall. Yellow PR waymarking. *IGN map 3742 OT*

Equipment: see page 9; stout shoes, sun protection, plan of Nice and information about the Colline du Château (from the tourist office).

Transport: city 🚌 14 from J-C Bermond (or any convenient stop) to the Mont Boron bus terminus; half-hourly in the week, hourly on week-ends; journey time about 30min

Refreshments: *no* refreshments available until you return to the port.

Points of interest:
Colline du Château
old forts
Old Nice
views!

Short walk: Mont Boron and Mont Alban. 4km/2.5mi; 1h 15min. Easy. Follow the main walk to the 1h15min-point, then take 🚌 14 back to the centre.

Start the walk at the **bus shelter** on **Mont Boron**. Walk to the **area map** at the far side of the square. Two paths face you here: take the tarred footpath to the left, the **Sentier du Cap de Nice**. This circles Mont Boron below the **old fort**, affording the fine views shown overleaf. Olive trees, holm oaks and pines shade the path-side benches. Soon views open out over Cap Ferrat (Walk 4) and its lighthouse.

When you come to a road, the path continues just to the left of it. But first cross the road, to another lovely viewpoint. Return to the path and follow it to a barrier. You are just 100m/yds short of your starting point, but it cannot be seen from here. Now take the trail that goes off left at a 90° angle, and walk round another barrier. This trail (**Circuit de Bellevue**) rounds the seaward side of the fort, circling the hill at a higher level.

When this second circuit is complete, go left on the road and

Nice from the Sentier du Cap de Nice

follow it in a curve to the right, back to the square with the bus shelter (**35min**).

Continue along the road past the **area map**, following signs for 'Auberge de la Jeunesse'. When the road curves right, take a tarred path off left (ignore the Allée du Bois Dormant just to the left of it). Rejoin the road and continue left uphill, quickly passing the **maison forestière** on the left. At a Y-fork go right for 'Fort du Mt Alban', then cut a bend off the road by walking left through a **picnic area**. In early spring this road is a blaze of yellow-flowering tree-spurge *(Euphorbia dendroides)*. From the **Fort du Mont Alban**

Woodland path on Mt Boron (left) and the fort on Mt Alban

(**55min**) the views down over Villefranche and its bay are superb.

Return the same way to the **area map** in the square on Mont Boron (**1h15min**). Now descend the concreted steps on the right (the **Chemin des Crêtes**). Keep straight downhill through mixed woodlands, accompanied by wrens and robins, crossing straight over roads. In 10 minutes you pass to the right of the richly-decorated modern church (1927) of **Notre-Dame du Perpétuel Secours**.

When you reach the Boulevard Carnot/N98 *cross carefully* (blind corners). The path continues just at the left side of the Hotel Marbella, heading towards the port and the Colline du Château. Make your way to the **Club Nautique** and continue opposite the **commercial port** along the lovely residential Boulevard Franck Pilatte (🚌 20, 30, 32b). Follow the road inland (signposted 'Gare'), but turn left after about 40m/yds and walk to the **pleasure port**. Circle the port on the quays, then turn left towards the Promenade des Anglais, quickly coming to the beautiful **memorial** to the dead of World Wars I and II on the right, its high arch carved into the **Colline du Château** (**2h**).

Keep rounding the hill, until you come to the lift (*ascenseur*), and pay the small fee to ride up to the top (or climb the adjacent steps; 90m/300ft). Allow a good half hour to potter about on the top of

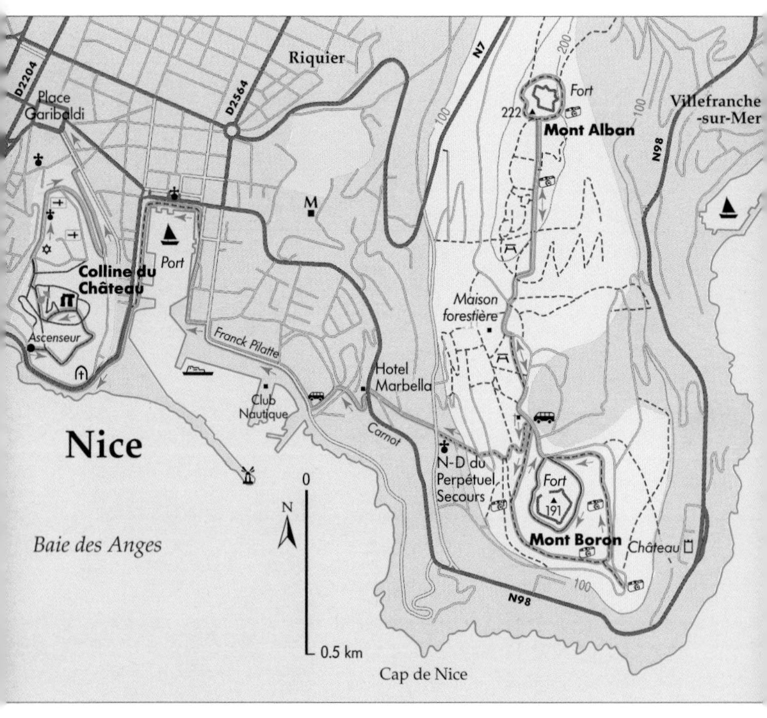

Colline du Château: foundations of the ruined cathedrals and artificial waterfall fed by the Vésubie River

the hill — not missing the Tour Bellanda (Naval Museum), the mosaics, the ruins of two cathedrals (10-12C and 14C) which once stood in the grounds of the Duke of Savoy's château, the beautiful waterfall fed by the Vésubie ... and the views!

To return to town you could take the lift or adjacent steps or pick up the tourist train. We usually walk down via the cemeteries: take the steps below the waterfall, down to a road. Turn right, then take steps on the left signposted **'Cimetières, Vielle Ville'**. From the lowest (Roman Catholic) cemetery, take the road downhill to the right, then make a sharp hairpin bend to the left on Montée Eberlé. This leads to the **Place Garibaldi** (**3h**; 7 on the town plan), from where you can explore Old Nice — and have some seafood at the Café de Turin (34) or a *socca* at René's (30).

Cafe de Turin

The place in Nice for fish — particularly shellfish — and conveniently located at Place Garibaldi (34 on the plan), where Walk 1 ends (also near the main bus station).

Everything from the popular sea bass to 10 varieties of oyster, even sea urchins in season. An institution; always full, ensuring the freshest of food. Very popular take-away business.

CAFE DE TURIN
5 Place Garibaldi ✆ 04 93 62 29 52
daily all year from 08.00-23.00
€-€€€

huge menu with dozens of different **fish** dishes prepared to order – grilled, baked, poached, sauced

oysters a speciality

seasonal seafood platters: Atlantic lobster and crab, crayfish, snails, prawns, mussels, etc

for those who don't fancy seafood there are meat dishes and even pizza and socca

René Socca

If you want to try *socca,* Nice's speciality dish, it's best to go to Old Nice, where it's widely available. We've been told that the best *socca* in the old town is to be had at **Chez Pipo** (13 Rue Bavastro, ✆ 04 93 55 88 82), but it's only open in the evenings (17.00-22.00 Tue-Sun, also Mon in Jul/Aug). We haven't tried it, because we prefer *socca* for lunch. (If you *do* go, get there early — waiting time for a table can be an hour or so!)

Our favourite place is **René Socca** (30); it has the advantage of being just a couple of hundred yards from the bus station *(gare routière),* at the top of Rue Pairolière, mentioned on page 18. There's a secret or two to eating at René's, because it is so busy!

It's a simple place — an open-fronted shop on the corner of Rue Pairolière and Rue Mirhaletti, surrounded by thick wooden tables

restaurants

TURI
SONT PAS ACCEPTES

RENE SOCCA
2, Rue Mirhaletti (04 93 92 05 73
daily ex Mon from 09.00-21.00 €

socca (chick-pea 'pancake')

petits farcis (stuffed courgettes, onions, peppers)

pizza and **pissaladière** (pizza with onion, black olives and ancovy)

deep-fried **courgette flowers**

aubergine and **courgette** fritters

cabillaud (spicy fritters made from dried cod – Fridays only)

fritures (whitebait)

sardines and lemon

daube (beef stew) with polenta

pan bagnat (thick sandwich; the bread is moistened with olive oil and vinegar)

tourte de blettes (chard pie)

sweet *tartes* (apple, etc)

and benches. Of course in Nice it's usually pleasant to eat outdoors, but if it's too sunny, too cold or raining, there is also *indoor seating* (most visitors don't realise this). The entrance to the indoor dining room is opposite the *socca* window.

Rene's sells far more than *socca*, and here's our second tip. The *socca* is sold from the window on Rue Mirhaletti; all the other food is sold from Rue Pairolière. *There are two queues, and the socca queue is by far the longer* — it stretches round the block into Rue Pairolière, so you have to try to find where it ends! Keep approaching *local* people with the word *'socca'*; if they nod, they are in the *socca* queue...

So the strategy is this: one person queues for the food, while the other(s) find a table and order the drinks (*it is compulsory to buy something to drink if you are sitting at any table, indoors or out*).

If you are *only* having *socca*, make for the *socca* queue. But why not try some of Rene's other specialities (as the French family below are doing)? Admittedly, the dozens of dishes stacked up in the main window look cold and rather unappealing, but as soon as you have chosen (just point to what you want), they heat it up for you.

By this time you should have moved round to the *socca* window, and the *socca* should be served in a trice, as it's coming out of the fires every few minutes. *Petits farcis* and *fritures* go especially well with *socca.* And rosé wine (by the glass) is the preferred drink of the locals, although there is also Normandy cider and beer.

As you can imagine, René's also has a very popular take-away service.

SOCCA AND *PETITS FARCIS*

Socca

This recipe requires a *very* hot oven, which must be preheated to the highest setting available *for one hour.* Just before placing the socca in the oven, change setting to grill.

Put 0.5 l of water and the olive oil in a bowl, add the flour gradually, and whisk until there are *no* lumps (strain if necessary). Season with salt and pepper.

Spread in a thin layer (2-3 mm) on a heavily greased baking tray and place just below the grill. Heat until dark gold (5min) — or even slightly burnt. Scrape into servings and season with freshly ground black pepper.

All too much work? An easier method is to prepare the batter and fry like a pancake.

Ingredients (for 4 people)

250 g chick-pea (gram) flour
2 tbsp olive oil
salt, freshly-ground black pepper

Stuffed vegetables (*petits farcis*)

Preheat the oven to 180°C, 350°F, gas mark 4. Cut the vegetables into quarters. Scoop out all the flesh and set it aside. If you are using cooked, leftover meat, poach the vegetables for about 8 minutes.

Mince the vegetable innards and mix together with the meat, eggs, garlic, parsley and cheese. Season to taste.

Fill the vegetable 'shells' with the stuffing, sprinkle the top with breadcrumbs and drizzle with olive oil. Bake for only 15-20 minutes if using pre-poached vegetables and pre-cooked meat. Otherwise bake for 30-35 minutes.

The *farcis* may be eaten either hot or cold. At René's the meat used is mostly ham, but some recipes call for minced steak, others veal or chicken. There's no reason why you shouldn't use any stuffing – or indeed vegetables – of your choice, as long as the proportions are right.

Ingredients (for 4 people)

2 large red peppers
2 large onions
2 small aubergines
2 medium courgettes
500 g mild sausage meat or any mince or minced leftovers you fancy
2 cloves garlic, minced
2 eggs, beaten
50 g grated parmesan
fresh parsley
salt and pepper to taste
breadcrumbs (optional)
olive oil

The flanks of Mont Chauve ('Bald Mountain') are virtually treeless, so all along this invigorating ridge walk you'll have unimpeded views. The sense of isolation is wonderful, too; it's hard to believe you're at the edge of the Riviera — until you take in the panorama from the massive fort!

mont chauve d'aspremont

WALK 2

The bus trip to Aspremont, weaving up narrow roads through the hinterland hill villages, is a highlight in itself — especially as you can use your city bus pass and travel 'free'! You'll have marvellous views up to the Mercantour and across the Var Valley … and you'll pass through Bellet, home to one of the smallest, oldest and highly prized vineyards in France.

Distance: 10.5km/6.5mi; 3h25min

Grade: moderate ascent of 345m/1130ft and descent of 530m/1740ft. Good, but stony, paths and tracks underfoot. *Almost no shade.* Red and white GR, yellow PR waymarking. *IGN map 3742 OT*

Equipment: see page 9; sun protection, snacks and drinks

Transport: city 🚌 62 from J-C Bermond to Aspremont at 12.10 (Mon-Sat); journey time 45min; or city 🚌 76 from Le Ray (08.45, 11.20, 12.35 Mon-Sat); return on city 🚌 25 (17.20, 18.05, 18.40, 19.40 Mon-Sat).

Refreshments: Aspremont (at the start), Aire St-Michel (at the end, *but this may be closed*); *none en route*

Points of interest:
fort on the summit of Mt Chauve
views north and south

Alternative walk: Aspremont circuit. 8km/5mi; 2h40min. Grade as above (ascent/descent of 345m/1130ft). Access as above; return on city 🚌 76 at 16.40, 17.20, 18.05, 18.40, 19.40 (Mon-Sat). Notes on page 38.

Start out at the **bus stop/car park** in **Aspremont**. Walk towards Nice on the D14, but quickly turn right down the **Chemin de la Vallière** (GR waymarks), taking concrete steps down into the **Magnan Valley**. Meet the D14 again in five minutes and go straight over, up a lane. In two minutes keep ahead on a stony path. At a fork above an isolated house (**10min**), turn sharp right uphill on the GR5. (The path straight ahead is the GR51, the return route for the Alternative walk.)

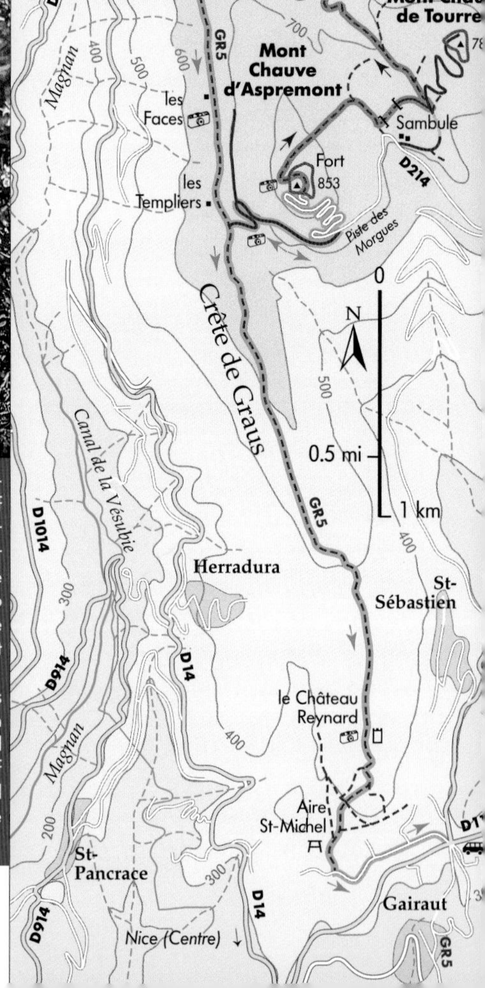

On the way up to Fondalin in the first part of the walk, watch out for the colonies of juniper bushes. If the berries are ripe (very dark blue to black), take some home to flavour your roast lamb.
Descending from Les Templiers at the high point of the walk, you'll come upon clusters of rosemary bushes. All year round the leaves are suitable for picking.

View north from Aspremont, in spring, with the Var Valley and the Mercantour mountains in cloud.

Rising on this stony path, you enjoy a fine view back over Aspremont on its conical hill and to the perched villages of Le Broc and Carros on the far side of the Var. Soon you pass a ruined building, **Fondalin (35min)**, in a very pleasant, grassy setting. The path rises gently through golden grasses and *garrigues* until, when you are above Nice's crematorium on the main road, the sea comes into view ahead.

Les Faces (50min) is the next little ruin on route. Rising below abandoned hillside terracing, you come to a final ruin

In spring the path is brilliantly green and gold, but the high mountains may be obscured by mist.

(**Les Templiers**; **1h**) and reach a fork 200m/yds further on. Leave the GR here: turn sharp left uphill on a cart track, now following yellow waymarks and enjoying some fine views down over Nice and the coast. On approaching a rock face, follow the track in a U-bend to the left and then a sharp turn to the right (where a track goes straight ahead, back towards Les Faces). The observatory on Mont Gros, as well as Mont Alban, Mont Boron and the port (Walk 1) are focal points on this stretch. The track contours above the rock face, with a fine view to the right along the Crête de Graus — the ridge you will follow back to Nice.

Exploring the fort and its 'moat' can be really creepy on a foggy day, but all the more fun for that!

On meeting a road (**Piste des Morgues**; **1h15min**), follow it uphill in tight hairpin bends to the summit of **Mont Chauve** (**1h35min**). The massive old **fort** here, the last in a line of coastal defences stretching from Ste-Agnès (Walk 7) to Nice, is one of the best viewpoints in the area. While the coastal views are mesmerising, don't forget to look back north — up towards the Mercantour and the Alps! Take time, too, to walk down around the grassy 'moat' between the inner and outer walls.

From the fort retrace your steps to the GR5 (**2h15min**). Now follow it to the left along the **Crête de Graus**. A slight rise takes you up to a **col** in about 35 minutes; ignore any minor or crossing paths, keep heading along the main path, towards a pylon. The path descends to the ruined walls of the **Château Reynard** (**3h**), a shady spot from where there is another fine view. The descent now becomes more pronounced for a short time, then levels out and comes to a T-junction. Go left, towards another pylon. At the pylon, *ignore* the yellow PR route straight ahead; go right on the GR, which then turns left on a wide crossing path, into the olive groves and pines of a picnic area with tables (**Aire St-Michel**). On meeting a lane, follow it downhill past villas, to a **bus shelter** on **Avenue Jules Romains** (**3h25min**).

Alternative walk: Aspremont circuit. Follow the main walk to the **fort (1h25min)**. The return path to Aspremont leaves from the northwest side of the outer wall (yellow waymark). *Watch carefully for the yellow waymarks* on this narrow goats' path which descends through broom, lavender and thyme, heading towards the houses of Sambule below. (If the waymarks have faded, refer to the map: just head northeast cross-country towards Mont Chauve de Tourette until you pick up the wide crossing path 0.5km downhill, where you turn right. Or, if it is foggy, go back down the Piste des Morgues and head left to Sambule. Walk through the hamlet, and take the signposted and waymarked path from there.)

At a wide crossing path, turn right, then keep downhill until you come to a **tunnel** on the left (**1h55min**). Walk through it (no torch needed) and exit looking straight across to the neighbouring (ruined) fort, **Tourrette**. Head right on a gravel track and turn left on another track after 200m/yds. At the Y-fork that follows almost immediately, bear left. When you come to a yellow arrow pointing up to the right, *ignore it;* keep ahead on the lovely grassy path, now making straight for Aspremont. Keep left again at the next Y-fork. Some 500m/yds further on, the path deteriorates and zigzags downhill over skiddy rubble. When you meet a cart track, turn left. On coming to a lane (**Chemin de la Bergerie**), follow it to the left. This takes you back to the GR51 path, which you follow back to **Aspremont (2h40min)**.

Hostellerie d'Aspremont

Walkers are assured a very friendly welcome in this small homely hotel. There's even a place to clean your boots!

The building was once a farm and is one of the oldest in the village. There's an open fire in the dining room in winter; in summer you'll want to eat out on the terrace — from where the views are *almost* as wonderful as from the walk itself! As you can see from the menu, local cuisine is the keynote.

Should the *hostellerie* be closed, Chez Mireille opposite also has fine views — or try Le Garrigou just by the bus stop.

At the end of the walk there is a very pleasant-looking inn opposite the bus stop, the **Auberge de l'Aire St-Michel**. Unfortunately, we've only seen it in winter, when it's been closed — with no information about opening dates or menu.

HOSTELLERIE D'ASPREMONT
Place St-Claude ✆ 04 93 08 00 05
www.cote.azur.fr/hotel_hostellerie-d-aspremont-aspremont_114.htm
closed January and Wed, Thu €-€€

three set menus are offered (all the same price); these will certainly vary from year to year; in 2004:

menu 1
salade niçoise
lamb stew Provençal-style (with tomatoes, onions, garlic, etc)

menu 2
fish soup Nice-style
chicken with crayfish sauce

menu 3
panned mussels, scallops and mushrooms
lamb skanks with thyme

all menus with **cheese** and **sweet**

MILK-FED LAMB

Milk-fed lamb is a speciality of the hill country above Nice. This recipe is an ideal way to end the day if you've just come back from the Aspremont walk with some fresh juniper berries and rosemary! Our recipe calls for *gin,* but there is no reason why you should not use wine instead.

Legs of lamb *(agneau)* are just one of the eye-catching displays at this butcher's stall in the Marché de la Buffa.

Around Easter milk-fed lamb *(agneau de lait)* is widely available in Nice, even in supermarkets. At other times you may have to order it in advance. But really, any nice leg of spring lamb will do.

A problem may be what size leg to buy. We usually just buy just half a leg (as in the photograph opposite, cooked at home using a British-cut half leg), but to serve four people generously, buy a whole leg (and use the leftovers for stew or soup). So, although our photograph shows a *half* leg of lamb, the recipe is for a *whole* leg.

Roast leg of lamb with juniper, garlic and rosemary

Preheat the oven to 190°C, 375°F, gas mark 5. Rub the lamb all over, *lightly,* with olive oil. Make small incisions in the meat and insert slivers of garlic, distributing them evenly. Tuck the juniper berries and rosemary in the same 'pockets'.

Place in a roasting pan and insert a meat thermometer (if you have one). Roast for 20-25min, or until the meat starts to brown. Now pour over the gin (or wine), and continue roasting, basting once or twice, until the meat thermometer registers 140° for medium-rare. Total cooking time should be 2-1/2h but, if you prefer your lamb pink, it should be done in 2h.

Let the meat sit for 10min before carving and add the meat juices to the pan — you may want to boil them up for a few minutes to scrape up all the crunchy bits and reduce. Serve with simple roast potatoes or potato 'cake' (see page 60) and perhaps fresh peas.

Ingredients (for 6-8 people)

2.5 kg leg of lamb *(gigot d'agneau)*
4 gloves garlic, slivered
12 or more juniper berries (either dried, or fresh but ripe)
fresh rosemary
150 ml gin (or wine)
salt, freshly ground pepper
olive oil

3

Old trails — some dating from Roman times — are followed in this circuit via the exquisite perched villages of Peillon and Peille. Which will you prefer? Peille thrills with its *via ferrata;* Peillon is picture-postcard perfect … and home to the Auberge de la Madone!

peillon and peille WALK

Distance: 11.5km/7.1mi; 3h35min

Grade: moderate ascents/descents of about 500m/1640ft overall. Little shade on the outgoing path, plenty on the return. Good yellow PR waymarking from Peillon, poor waymarking from Peille. *IGN map 3742 OT*

Equipment: see page 9; sun protection, walking stick

Transport: 🚆 to Peillon. Or 🚌 to Peille (there won't be time for the whole circuit; see 'Alternative routes' below).

Refreshments: bar, restaurants in Peille; *not always open* (Le Belvédère: ☎ 04 93 79 90 45; Chez Nana: ☎ 04 93 79 90 41); Auberge de la Madone at Peillon (see page 48)

Points of interest:

Peille village, its church with Romanesque belfry, and the *via ferrata*

Peillon village, the square, and the White Penitents' Chapel

Alternative routes: Peillon council has waymarked the **Circuit de Lourquière** and the **path from Peillon to La Grave de Peille.** You could take 🚌 116 to Peille (10.45 Mon-Sat), do the walk *in reverse* to Peillon (via the St-Pancrace Chapel and the Galambert Stream; well waymarked), have lunch at the Auberge de la Madone, then descend to La Grave (🚌 360 or 🚆 at 18.30).

Start out at the 18th-century **fountain** in **Peillon**. Walk up the paved steps behind it, then turn left at a signpost for 'Peille Village 2h'). You pass an **iron cross** and come into olive groves, with the **Lourquière** mountain rising on the right. At a first fork, keep ahead for 'Peille Village' and at the next go right (same sign). There is a beautiful view back to the thimble-like spur of Peillon now, and the path enters a gorge. When a **metal gate** blocks the path (**10min**), turn *sharp left* uphill.

Eventually the old stone-laid trail passes below the red-hued climbing rocks of the **Baus Roux**, then crosses the **Galambert Stream** on a **first stone bridge** (**30min**). Four minutes later, ignore a path forking back to the right; keep ahead. Ignore another path off right and keep ahead over a **second stone bridge** (**40min**;

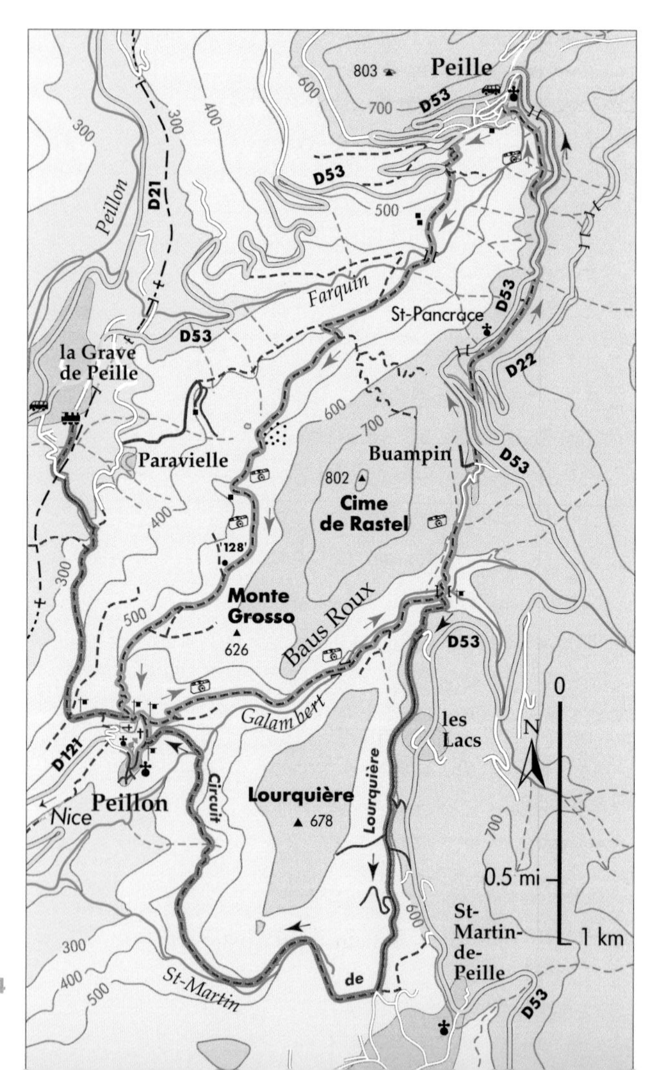
Peille
803
700
600
D53
400
300
500
Peillon
D21
Farquin
St-Pancrace
D22
la Grave
de Peille
Paravielle
Buampin
802
Cime
de Rastel
'128'
Monte
Grosso
626
Baus Roux
D53
Galambert
les
Lacs
D121
Peillon
Nice
Circuit
Lourquière
678
Lourquière
0
0.5 mi
1 km
N
St-
Martin-
de-
Peille
de
St-Martin
D53

The *via ferrata* where it spans Peille's gorge

sign: 'Chapelle St-Pancrace, Peille'). Continue uphill, straight towards the masts on the Cime de la Morgelle (but this 1076m-high peak rises well to the east of your ongoing route). Tar comes underfoot in **Buampin** (**50min**): keep uphill until the road curves right, then walk straight ahead alongside the fence of a **builders' yard** on your left. At a fork 20m/yds along, keep right; continue across a driveway and up to the D53 (**1h**).

Follow the road to the left for 200m/yds and, at the junction with the D22, turn sharp right. Walk up the D22 for 150m/yds, then turn hard back left on a path (cairn). This pretty path passes the ruined **Chapelle St-Pancrace**, then descends gently through pines, back to the D53. Follow the road to the right. When the road bends right, by a rock promontory on the left (**1h25min**), your ongoing path dives down left just *before* the

Peille's cluster of rose-hued buildings

rock promontory. ***Note:*** *this path is badly eroded, with unprotected drops to the left; you will get to Peille almost as quickly by continuing along the D53 — a safer option.*

The path (or the road) gives you some superb views of Peille's pride and joy: its well-engineered *via ferrata* — climbing walls with iron hand-holds and suspension bridges over the dramatic **Farquin Gorge**. After crossing a stone bridge, the path rises to the **museum** at **Peille** (**1h45min**).

Once you've wandered around this beautifully-sited village strung out along the ravine walls, make your way to the round tower of the ***hôtel de ville*** and descend the adjacent steps (**Rue des Pous**). Keep zigzagging almost due south for about 10 minutes, until you reach the **final hairpin bend of the** D53 below Peille, where your ongoing path descends concrete steps at the left (yellow and blue paint waymarks; **2h**).

At a fork reached very quickly, take the descending path to the right (with a water pipe on your left). Keep downhill across traces of hunters' paths, passing to the left of some houses in 10 minutes and crossing the **Farquin Stream** five minutes later (**2h15min**). *From here follow the notes carefully;* it is easy to get lost in these beautiful, dense oak woods, as *all the paths are* *waymarked in yellow!* Rise up from the bridge, in five minutes ignoring a path back to the right. Pass to the left of a huge boulder which bears some yellow and red waymarks. Ten minutes up from the bridge, ignore a large cairn on the right but, three minutes later, another tall cairn marks an ***important junction, where you must turn sharp left.*** (The path straight ahead eventually joins a track, then descends to Paravielle and La Grave de Peille.) ***Two minutes later, at a Y-fork, keep right.*** In 10 minutes the path curls round to the right at the foot of a very large **scree** (**2h40min**). *If you have not reached this point within 30 minutes from crossing the Farquin Stream, you have gone wrong.* Ten minutes later the path runs through pines and tall grass higher up the ridge — a very attractive setting. You pass to the left of a building (**2h55min**), then curl left towards the crests. As you push through masses of broom *(this stretch can be very overgrown in spring),* there are some open views down right to the huge quarry at La Grave.

Rise to a **col and marker stone 128** on the right (**3h05min**); keep straight ahead here, ignoring a path back to the right. Seven minutes later, at a Y-fork, keep right, quickly passing to the right of a cairn. From here the path descends gently, eventually coming to a fork: keep straight ahead (sign: 'Peillon Village'). A stone-laid trail takes you to the next fork, where you go right (same sign). At a third fork, keep straight on, retracing your steps past the **iron cross** to the **fountain** in **Peillon** (**3h35min**). Before leaving, be sure to visit the **Chapelle des Pénitents Blancs** with its Renaissance frescoes — and perhaps enjoy some refreshments at the Auberge de la Madone.

Auberge de la Madone

This family-run hotel and restaurant is praised in all the up-market guides. Father and son do the cooking; vegetables and herbs come

Hot chocolate on the terrace at the Auberge de la Madone, March

AUBERGE DE LA MADONE
Place Auguste-Arnulf, Peillon
✆ 04 93 79 91 17
www.chateauxhotels.com/madone
closed Wed, 7-31 Jan, 20 Oct-20 Dec €€€

luncheon menu at 30 € (main course, dessert, glass of wine); *not available on Sun/holidays*

eight different **entrées** — like broad bean soup with savoury, new onions, fresh cows' cheese and lightly grilled mountain ham

nine **main courses**, ranging from **fish** (fried fillets of red mullet with a compote of tomatoes, tiny purple artichokes and the juice of Menton lemons) to **poultry** (roasted farm-raised guinea fowl on a polenta base, with fig and cherry sauce) to **meat** (milk-fed lamb cooked in the traditional way)

small but intriguing **cheese board**

eight different **desserts** — like nougat ice cream with honey and grilled caramelized almonds

from their own garden. This is fine cuisine and best sampled at leisure.

Treat yourself! Take a bus to Peille, walk to Peillon, laze about over lunch then amble down to La Grave de Peille for a bus or train. *But be sure to reserve a table in advance!*

Alternatively, start your day with a steaming mug of hot chocolate or coffee on their terrace — or end it here with afternoon tea.

CHRISTMAS-DAY PHEASANT

As amateur cooks, we're unable to duplicate any of the Madone recipes, but writing about Peillon reminds us of a wonderful dinner we enjoyed after doing Walk 3 one Christmas Day. We'd bought our pheasant the day before from the Buffa market.

Preheat the oven to 190°C, 375°F, gas mark 5.

In a heavy casserole (the one you will use for the oven), brown the pheasant pieces in the butter, then remove. Put in the onions and cook them until translucent.

Return the pheasant to the casserole and pour over *half* the brandy. Set alight and, when the flame subsides, add the stock, juniper berries, salt and pepper. Bring just to the boil, then cook in the preheated oven, covered, for about 45min.

Remove the pheasant, but keep it warm. Boil up the juices until they reduce, then add the rest of the brandy, the cream and the lemon juice. Let simmer (not boil) until you have a syrupy sauce.

If you've had time to make it, potato 'cake' (see page 60) is a treat with this dish.

Ingredients (for 4 people)

2 pheasants (ask the butcher to clean and joint for you)
1 medium onion, chopped
40 g butter
200 ml beef stock
150 ml cream
6 juniper berries
120 ml brandy (or whisky)
salt and pepper to taste
1/2 tsp lemon juice

Lovely any time of year, this walk is especially enjoyable on a bright and bracing winter's day. You'll walk below the exotic gardens of some of the most exquisite properties on the Riviera, with far-reaching views out to sea and for miles east and west along the 'Azure Coast'.

around cap ferrat

WALK 4

Begin the walk overlooking the **port** at **St-Jean-Cap-Ferrat**. Walk south, then east, round the port, then go up **Avenue Jean Mermoz**, keeping the Hotel Voile d'Or on your left. Take steps on the left down to the **Paloma Beach** restaurant. Here you pick up a coastal walkway running round the **Pointe de St-Hospice**, with fine views over to Eze, La Turbie, the Tête de Chien, Monaco and Cap Martin.

After rounding the point, take steps on the right (sign) up to the 19th-century **Chapelle St-Hospice** with its huge bronze-painted statue of Virgin and Child. An 18th-century **tower** is adjacent, but is on private land and not fully visible.

Then return to the coastal path and turn right. Beyond the **Pointe du Colombier**, the path enters a lovely pine

Distance: 8km/5mi; 2h45min

Grade: easy, with ups and downs of about 130m/425ft, *but potentially dangerous when wet or very windy.* Adequate shade. No waymarks, but easily followed. *IGN map 3742 OT*

Equipment: see page 9; swimming things, sun protection

Transport: city 🚌 81 from the main bus station *(gare routière)* to Le Port de St-Jean (09.10, 09.40, 10.15, 10.55, 11.30 Mon-Sat); journey time 30min; returns 15.30, 16.20, 16.45, 17.45, 18.10, 19.00, 19.25, 20.15; or 🚗

Refreshments: bars, cafés and restaurants at St-Jean (start/end)

Points of interest:
Chapelle St-Hospice
beautifully built coastal path and adjacent properties
Ephrussi de Rothschild Foundation/Ile de France Museum (paid entrance)

Alternative walk: Start or end at **Beaulieu**, served every 15 minutes by Menton buses from the *gare routière* (and frequent trains). 10.5km/6.5mi; 3h20min. Grade as main walk. A seafront walkway (the **Promenade Maurice-Rouvier**) runs between the casino/marina at Beaulieu and St-Jean-Cap-Ferrat. Follow it either way to extend the walk; the Villa Kerylos is en route.

La Pinède (left) and view up to the lighthouse; below: stained-glass window at the Chapelle St-Hospice

wood (**La Pinède**) at the edge of a little bay (**Les Fossettes**), then meets a road at a T-junction (**1h**). Turn left here (a right turn leads back to the port). Follow the road past the next little bay, **Les Fosses**.

At the next T-junction, eight minutes later, go left and walk round a metal barrier. You pick up the coastal walkway again and begin to round **Cap Ferrat**. Trailing superb views inland (and dodging the sea-spray), now you can really stride out, while watching the yachts and high-speed ferries sailing to and from the nearby ports of Villefranche and Nice.

The path passes above many pretty little inlets, and below

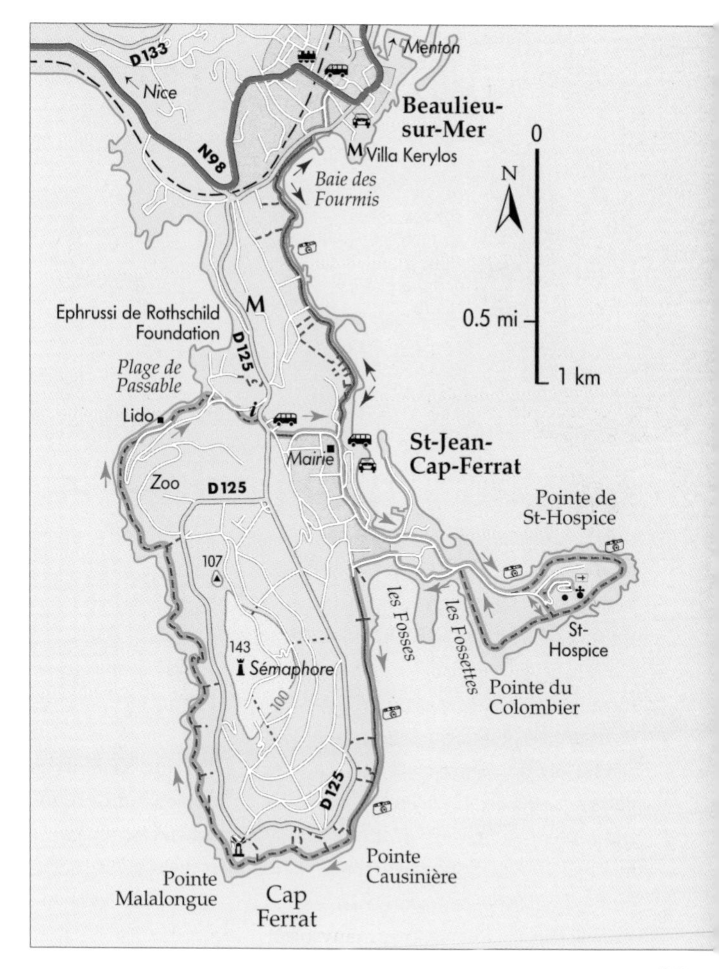
D133
Menton
Nice
Beaulieu-
sur-Mer
N98
Villa Kerylos
Baie des
Fourmis
N
0
0.5 mi
1 km
Ephrussi de Rothschild
Foundation
D125
Plage de
Passable
Lido
St-Jean-
Cap-Ferrat
Mairie
Zoo
D125
Pointe de
St-Hospice
107
les Fosses
les Fossettes
St-
Hospice
143
Sémaphore
100
Pointe du
Colombier
D125
Pointe
Causinière
Pointe
Malalongue
Cap
Ferrat

Port at St-Jean-Cap-Ferrat; in the background are the cliffs descended in Walk 6, with the Tête de Chien prominent on the far right.

the **lighthouse** (**1h40min**; paid entrance, if you decide to climb up to it).

After skirting the Lido apartments by road, the path ends at the **Plage de Passable** (**2h30min**). Climb the steps at the left of the beachside restaurant, cross straight over a road and go up more steps. At the next road, walk left for 160m/yds, then go right, up an alley. You emerge on the main D125 (**Avenue Denis Séméria**); the **tourist office** is on your left. Walk to the **bus shelter** opposite (to the right) and take another alley just to the right of it. Rejoining Avenue Séméria lower down, follow it against the one-way traffic back to the **port** at **St-Jean**. A bus stop is opposite the **mairie** (**2h45min**), and there are cafés and restaurants galore, several of them open in winter.

There are dozens of restaurants in Cap Ferrat and nearby Beaulieu, ranging from 5-star to smaller bistros, *crêperies* and ice cream parlours. Many of the restaurants beside the port at St-Jean are open all year round and, if the day is fine, this is where everyone congregates to enjoy the lively atmosphere.

CAPITAINE COOK
11, Avenue Jean-Mermoz
✆ 04 93 76 02 66
closed all day Wed, Thu lunch, and 8 Nov-26 Dec €€

menus at 23 € and 27 €

the **speciality** is all kinds of seafood, prepared in myriad ways

but there are **poultry** and **meat dishes**, like half chicken with mushrooms in a cream sauce, slivered calves liver with shallots, guinea fowl *(pintadeau)*, lamb fricassee, and various steaks

If you want to dine with the stars, then *the* place to be seen is **Le Sloop** (✆ 04 93 01 48 63; closed Wed in winter and from 15 Nov to 20 Dec; reservations recommended). This is a beautifully decorated *restaurant gastronomique,* but with a lunch menu at only 27 €.

Another popular place, *not* on the harbour, is passed just near the start of the walk — **Capitaine Cook**, a long-standing seafood restaurant with a very pretty vine-covered terrace and cosy interior with some interesting paintings. It's on your left, just past the Voile d'Or. Rumour has it that it was the inspiration for the film *Casablanca* — in the 1930s it had a pianist called Sam.

There is also the informal restaurant at **Paloma Beach**, which you cross early on, but it's only open from May to September.

We sometimes go to St-Jean early in the morning and have breakfast before setting out — perhaps at **Le Croissant** (open all year from 08.00; huge, varied breakfast menu from 7,50 €). Then, if it's winter (our favourite time of year to walk here) and the harbourside isn't at its scintillating best, we repair back to our base restaurant in Nice.

Le Pot d'Etain — our base restaurant

Like so many of our favourite restaurants, we discovered this one many years ago. We wanted a base restaurant for *dinner,* one not more than a 10-minute walk from the centre/pedestrian area/Promenade des Anglais. That ruled out Old Nice — too far to walk home after a bottle (or more) of wine.

An important consideration was the *range* of dishes — some evenings we might fancy a gourmet meal, others just soup or an omelette. But for us the most important point of all was: could we trust the cooking?

One evening we ventured into Rue Meyerbeer and spied a chalked menu board featuring grilled *loup de mer*. Although the interior looked a bit up-market for a *base* restaurant, the 'menu' prices were reasonable. It turned out to be a most memorable meal, accompanied by Michèle's potato cake and wonderfully tart salad greens. Alas, fish no longer figures on the menu; most people come for steak or duck and, since she buys in fresh every day, there was too much waste.

Le Pot d'Etain (31 on the plan) is a classic French restaurant with a very comfortable, relaxed atmosphere, featuring several specialities from southwestern France. The basic menu *(carte)* is limited, but caters for just what we want, from salads to gourmet dishes. The chalk-board sug-

restaurants

eat

LE POT D'ETAIN
12 Rue Meyerbeer
(04 93 88 25 95
dinner only, Mon-Sat; closed the first two weeks of Jan €€

daily **menu** of different dishes — varying according to season

specialities of the house are cassoulet (recipe page 59), duck and *pâté de foie gras*

entrees include a beautiful plate of pork terrine, *foie gras* and smoked duck breast served with home-made relishes (*assiette gourmande;* see photo), **omelette with truffles**, **fish soup**

steaks are out of this world — with or without ceps (large wild mushrooms); **rack of lamb** (for two)

good, if quite limited, selection of **cheeses**, beautifully served with roquette or mesclun

just a few fabulous **desserts** — like **chocolate cake** (see page 61)

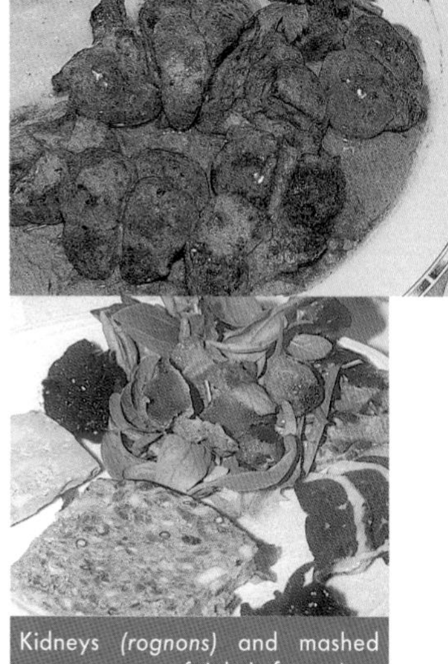

Kidneys *(rognons)* and mashed potato — one of John's favourites; below: *assiette gourmande* (see left; here served with ceps as well)

gestions vary by the week, adding plenty of variety. (But in season Pat will still have the courgette flowers *every* night!) We visit so regularly that we often have just one course — or share a couple of courses, so that we can enjoy the superb cooking without being overwhelmed by too much rich food ... or breaking the bank.

Of course for us the greatest advantage is that we *trust the cooking*. John can revel in *rognons* or one of the exquiste steaks; the delicious sauces are achieved by reduction, *not* by thickening with flour. So if you have dietary needs, just make them known to Michèle in advance and say we sent you.

CASSOULET DE CASTELNAUDARY

This is just one of many possible recipes for the most traditional and authentic of all cassoulets. One of La Mère Besson's favourite winter warmers (see page 66), 'Family-style cassoulet', called for shoulder of lamb instead of duck! At home we make a very quick 'cheat's cassoulet' of (tinned) butter beans, bacon bits, and sausages in a Bovril-enriched gravy. It's delicious.

For the recipe below (which takes some time), it's important to use the best ingredients. French *confits* should be used (available back home in some supermarket chains and in specialist shops). Don't try making your own *confits* — the legs of British ducks and geese are not as fat and succulent as those reared in France. Similarly, the best dried beans are those from Tarbes (*haricots tarbais,* with their own 'appellation controlée!) or *haricots lingots* (a long, white, slightly curved haricot bean).

Soak the beans overnight in cold water. The next day, change the water let them boil for 30min, keeping an eye on the water to make sure they are always covered. Then drain the beans and preheat the oven to 150°C, 300°F, gas mark 2.

In a heavy bottomed frying pan, bring together the goose grease, oil, tomatoes, onions and garlic cloves, and cook over a low heat for 10min. Set this mixture aside. Then put the 6 *confits* into the pan and heat (again on a very low fire) until all the fat has melted. Remove the meat and set aside; leave the fat in the pan.

Using the fat from the *confits,* put in the pork rind (if you have not been able to get this back home, use bacon bits sold in most super-

Michèle's cassoulet

markets) and cook until golden brown. Remove and set aside. Still using the same fat, put in the sausage and fry gently until browned all over.

Now put the tomato and onion mixture, the pork rind and the beans into an appropriately-sized casserole, together with one clove and a bouquet garni. Make sure it is all *just* covered with water. Add some pepper to taste, but *not* salt (the pork is already salty enough). Put the casserole in the oven for 1h30min. Keep watch as it cooks — the idea is to keep it topped up with enough water to *just* cover the ingredients.

After this prelimiary cooking, tuck the *confits* into the beans near the bottom and the sausages into the beans near the top. Add more water if necessary, to *just* cover it all. Cook for one more hour, always keeping an eye on the water.

Serve bubbling hot, in the casserole itself. (Some recipes call for breadcrumbs to be sprinkled on top at the last minute and quickly browned under the grill.)

Ingredients (for 6 people)

1 kg dry haricots beans (preferably *tarbais* or *lingot*)
300 g tomatoes, peeled and deseeded)
1 tbsp goose grease *(graisse d'oie)*
2 tbsp groundnut oil
2 onions, chopped
6 garlic cloves
6 *confits de canard* (cooked duck, preserved in its fat)
500 g fresh Toulouse or garlic sausage
1 clove
100 g pork rind *(couennes)*
1 bouquet garni
pepper

TWO WAYS WITH CAKES!

When Michèle has time (less often now, since the twin grand-daughters were born), she makes the most marvellous potato cake. This is not her recipe, but as close an approximation as we could find. The chocolate cake recipe opposite *is* her own.

Potato cake *(gâteau aux pommes de terre)*

You will need a loose-bottomed cake tin 18 cm in diameter and 8-10 cm high. Preheat the oven to 220°C, 425°F, gas mark 7. Put aside four of the larger potatoes (to line the pan). Slice all the potatoes lengthwise, *as thinly as possible* (2-3 mm). Dry the slices on paper towels.

Ingredients (for 6-8 servings)

1 kg waxy Mediterranean-style potatoes, peeled
75 g butter, melted
salt and pepper

Brush the tin liberally with melted butter. Using the larger potatoes, cut a circle about 5 cm in diameter from one of the slices and set in the centre bottom of the tin. Then overlap slices all round it (see photo). Now line the edge of the tin, standing slices vertically, slightly overlapping, and making sure that about 10 mm is curled on top of the base slices (to seal the edges).

Carefully mix the rest of the potatoes with the butter, salt and pepper. Press them tightly into the tin. Cover the lot with foil and press down firrmly against the potatoes. Bake for 1h30min (pierce

with a skewer or knife to check that they are cooked). Let the cake rest for 10min before turning out *carefully,* by gently teasing the edges. Then lightly brush the top with butter and place under a pre-heated grill until golden and crisp. Good hot or cold!

Chocolate cake *(gâteau au chocolat)*

It only makes sense to make this delicious but very large cake when you're back home, since it freezes beautifully. You will need a non-stick loose-bottomed cake tin 25 cm in diameter at the bottom and *at least* 7 cm high (the cake rises quite a lot, before falling back in when cooled). The tin should be *liberally* greased with butter and *lightly* dusted with flour or corn flour. Preheat the oven to 200°C, 400°F, gas mark 6.

Melt the chocolate with the butter. Separate the eggs and beat the whites to form peaks. Mix the yolks with the sugar until the mixture just becomes white. Using a wooden spoon, stir in the butter/chocolate mixture. Then *gently* fold in the egg whites.

Ease the cake into the pan and cook for 25min. If at this point it is still 'wobbly', give it another five minutes. Refrigerate overnight before removing from the tin. Don't mind its lopsided appearance — that is part of its rustic charm!

Ingredients (about 16 servings)

10 eggs
250 g dark chocolate (at least 70% cocoa)
250 g white granulated sugar
250 g butter

This little gem takes you into the red-rock Esterel Massif, a mass of colour all year round. Strong walkers could extend the hike: the routes marked in violet on the map are all waymarked. We end at Théoule's most popular restaurant, but you *could* return to Nice via Cannes, to have a meal at the famous La Mère Besson.

5 WALK to the esterel

Distance: 12km/7.4mi; 3h30min from/to Théoule's railway station; 8km/5mi; 2h10min from the centre

Grade: easy; ascent/descent of 130m/425ft overall. Some of the tracks and paths are stony underfoot; little shade. Red and white GR, yellow PR waymarking. *IGN map 3544 ET*

Equipment: see page 9; swimming things, sun protection

Transport: 🚂 to Théoule-sur-Mer (09.00, 12.00 daily); journey time about 50min; returns at 16.15 (via Cannes), 17.42. 🚌 620 runs from Théoule to Cannes at 15.55, 16.25, 16.55, 17.55, 18.25, 18.55 (Mon-Sat); journey time 45min. Or 🚗 to Théoule

Refreshments: cafés and restaurants at Théoule-sur-Mer (start/end)

Points of interest:
Esterel Massif

Alternative walks: See violet lines on the map to rise to the GR51/Balcons de la Côte d'Azur and prolong the circuit.

Begin at the **railway station** for Théoule, 1km north of the village on the N98. While you *can* just follow the N98 south to Théoule from here, it's preferable to follow the GR51 signs from the station. The GR crosses the railway line 400m/yds south of the station and runs through a little valley, before returning to the N98 and coming into **Théoule-sur-Mer** (**40min**). Turn right off the N98 at signs for *'mairie, poste'*. Pass both (on your left) and keep straight ahead. When this street makes a hairpin turn to the left (back to the N98), continue ahead on a track (sign: 'Col de Théoule'), rising above the railway line, into the Esterel.

Just as the railway enters the **Tunnel des Saumes** (**1h10min**), be sure to turn off right, following the GR along a footpath below the track. This path then rises to the **Col de Théoule** (**1h30min**), a major crossroads. From the col, head southwest on a *footpath* between two tracks (sign: 'Esquillon'). The path heads straight towards the Pointe de l'Esquillon, eventually widening into a track. When you come to a road junction some 40m/130ft above the N98 (**2h**), turn left on a 'balcony' footpath and walk northeast, with fine coastal views, eventually passing above **Port-la-Galère**.

At a fork, keep right, continuing northeast above the N98 on a lane (you will pass a **chapel** on the right). As you approach the

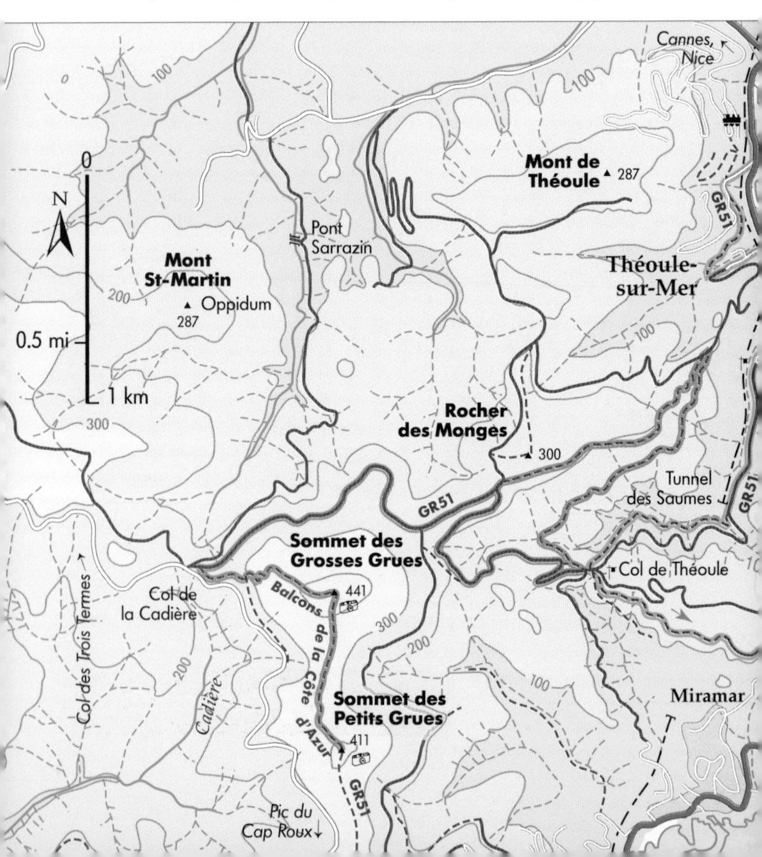

Pointe de l'Aiguille (where a park is up to the left; **2h35min**), cross the N98 and go down to the superb rock formations at the point. Then follow the coastal path from the point to **Théoule** (**2h50min**). You will emerge by the beachside **Marco Polo** restaurant (**bus shelter**; departures to Cannes shown on page 63). Or retrace your outgoing route back to the **station** (**3h30min**).

View to the Golfe de la Napoule from the Balcons de la Côte d'Azur (Alternative walk)

Marco Polo

Spoilt for choice! The walk ends at the very friendly, *very popular* **Marco Polo** restaurant (with seaside terrace). If you find yourselves too late for lunch (last orders 14.30) and too early for the train, take a bus into Cannes. Have an apéritif on the Croisette, then move on to one of the most famous restaurants on the Riviera.

MARCO POLO
47 Avenue des Lérins ✆ 04 93 49 96 59 closed Mon and 13 Nov-18 Dec; from 09.00 till 'late' €€ (1 menu at 29 €)

fish dishes of all kinds are the speciality (try the mixed seafood grill shown above, served with a lovely mayonnaise sauce), but there is **meat** as well, from duck to kid *(chevreau)* to steaks

morning **coffee**, afternoon **tea**, **snacks** and drinks all day

La Mère Besson

This restaurant opened in the 1930s and quickly became famous for authentic Provençal cooking — an 'in' place, especially during the Film Festival. Unfortunately, 'Mother' Besson is long dead, and current reviews are not always favourable. Judge for yourself! At least all the Mère Besson *recipes* in this book are authentic!

LA MERE BESSON
13 Rue des Frères Pradignac
✆ 04 93 39 59 24; open Mon-Sat all year, dinner only €-€€ (menus at 19 €, 27 €, 32 €)

daily **main-course specials**; Fridays are popular for the *aïoli* — a stew of desalted dried cod, vegetables and a creamy garlic *aïoli* sauce (see recipe on page 69)

Some of the dishes which made the restaurant famous include creamy **chicken with tarragon**, ***estouffade*** (braised beef in red wine with onions and mushrooms), ***bourride*** (fish stew; recipe overleaf), **shoulder of lamb** with Provençal herbs and garlic purée.

RECIPES FROM LA MERE BESSON

Chicken with tarragon and cream
(le poulet à l'estragon et à la crème)

Mère Besson's recipe (available on the current 19 € menu at the restaurant) calls for deboned chicken, but this is not necessary. If the chicken *is* deboned, reassemble the legs and wings with a wooden skewer or string. Put some of the tarragon leaves in boiling water for a few seconds, then rinse in cold water, drain and pat dry; add these at the last minute, thus retaining the colour.

In a frying pan just big enough to hold all the pieces, bring the oil to a high heat, then turn down a bit. Fry the chicken, turning, until just golden (about 6-7 minutes).

If there is any excess oil in the pan, pour it out. Add the wine, salt and pepper and tarragon. Let this cook gently for 20 minutes, partly covered, to reduce.

Now add the mushrooms and cream and let it reduce again – the sauce should be fairly thick. Best served with white rice.

Ingredients: (for 4 people)

1-1.2 kg chicken, cut up (and preferably deboned)
olive oil
3 sprigs fresh tarragon
150 ml dry white wine
100 ml crème fraîche
150 g button mushrooms, minced
salt and pepper to taste

Provençal fish stew *(bourride)*

This dish is a white *bouillabaisse*. If you start from scratch, it's a bit of a production! We've included both the full version and a 'cheat's version' of both the *court bouillon* and the *aïoli*. La Mère Besson's recipe did *not* call for potatoes or carrots, but we like it this way, and our cookery editor would add leeks and celery too!

Put the *court bouillon* and vegetables in a large heavy-bottomed pan. Cover, bring gently to the boil and cook gently for about 10min. When the vegetables are almost done, add the fish; cook for another 8-10min.

Put the fish and vegetables in a tureen or casserole and keep hot. Strain the *court bouillon* and, if necessary, add more water, until you have 600 ml of liquid. Whisk the egg yolks with a tiny bit of cold water into which you have dissolved the cornflour, then whisk in 150 ml of the *aïoli*. Pour on a little of the *court bouillon* and whisk together well.

Return to the heat and cook gently, stirring all the time, until the sauce thickens. *Do not let the sauce boil, or it will separate.* (If this should happen, you'll have to blend the sauce at high speed, strain it and reheat in a clean pan.)

Pour the sauce over the fish and vegetables. Put the bread or croutons in the bottom of (pre-warmed) soup bowls, and add some of the fish mixture. Pour over some of the sauce and garnish with fresh parsley. Serve the rest of the *aïoli* separately.

Ingredients: (for 4-6 people)

1 kg firm white fish, cut into large pieces
400 g waxy potatoes, cut into thick slices
150 g carrots, cut into thick chunks
300 ml *aïoli*
2 egg yolks
1 level tbsp cornflour
fresh parsley to garnish
toast or croutons to serve

-wood pestle and mortar:
ely and useful souvenir

For the *court bouillon*

Simmer together for 45min:
600 ml water, 150 ml white wine, 1 sliced onion, 1 sliced carrot, 1 sprig each of fennel, parsley and thyme, 1 bay leaf, 2 tbsp minced celery, 1 slice of lemon, 2 garlic cloves, 1 tsp salt and 6 black peppercorns. Then strain through a fine sieve.

OR just buy some fish stock, like Joubère, available in several UK supermarkets!

For the *aïoli* (garlic mayonnaise)

Set aside 300 ml olive oil. Crush together 4 garlic cloves and 1/4 tsp salt. Beat in 2 egg yolks. Add some oil, a few drops at a time, beating constantly. When this thickens, add 1 tbsp lemon juice. Slowly add the rest of the oil, beating, and 2 more tbsp lemon juice. Add pepper to taste.

OR simply crush the garlic with the salt, then stir into a really good, bought mayonnaise!

On this walk you will have some of the finest views on the whole of the Riviera. You rise gently along the north side of the Grande Corniche crest, with a superb outlook to the Mercantour mountains. After crossing the shoulder, you enjoy a magnificent coastal panorama for the whole of the plunging descent.

la turbie and èze

WALK 6

The walk begins at the *mairie* on the main road (D2564, the **Grande Corniche**) in **La Turbie**. Cross over the road to the Hotel Napoléon, then turn left. After 600m/yds, ignore the D2204 off right to the motorway; cross the wide junction and walk past a cylindrical **pillar with an iron cross** on the top and a builders' merchants (both on the right). At the end of the builders' perimeter fence, turn right up the **Chemin de la Forna** (**10min**; walkers' signpost). There are fine views back to the Trophée des Alpes as you climb.

As the tarmac runs out, keep straight ahead on a cart track (sign: 'Cime de la Forna'), to pass to the right of a **reservoir** (**20min**). Just before a second, square reservoir, turn left up another stony cart track (sign). In two minutes keep straight ahead

Distance: 8km/5mi; 3h15min

Grade: easy ascent of 155m/510ft, but strenuous descent of 600m/1970ft. Little shade. Yellow PR waymarking. *IGN map 3742 OT*

Equipment: see page 9; walking stick(s).

Transport: 🚌 116 from the main bus station *(gare routière)* to La Turbie (07.30, 10.45 Mon-Sat); journey time 40min; return by 🚌 100 (daily, very frequent) or 🚆 (15.57, 16.38, 17.17 Mon-Sat) from Eze-Bord-de-Mer

Refreshments en route: cafés and restaurants at La Turbie (start) and Eze Village (halfway)

Points of interest:

La Turbie and the Trophée des Alpes (see page 74)

Eze Village

Riviera views straight out of a film!

Shorter walk: La Turbie – Eze Village. 6km/3.7mi; 2h20min. Fairly easy, but a steep descent of 280m/920ft. Follow the main walk to Eze Village and return by city 🚌 82 at 15.30 or 17.15 (17.40 Sun). This avoids the final 320m/1050ft of descent.

Alternative walk: La Turbie circuit. 8.5km/5mi; 2h50min. Easy ascent as above. Access as above, or 🚗. Return: 🚌 116 (15.35, 18.00 Mon-Sat). See page 73 at 1h40min.

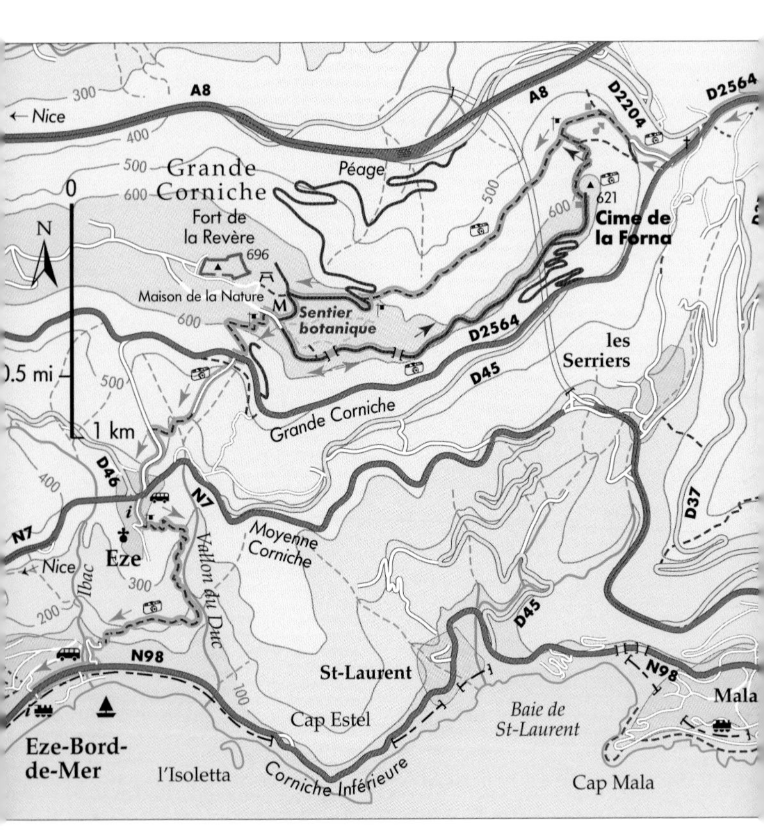

(sign: 'Fort de la Revère'). *(The Alternative walk returns via the 'Cime de la Forna' path to the left here.)*

Now a lovely path through tall grass takes you along the northern flanks of the **Grande Corniche**, just below the crest.

You look north to Utelle, where a chapel teeters on the edge of the cliff, and the mountains of the Mercantour. The Fort de la Revère crowns the rise to the west, above two forestry park buildings. From here the frenetic jockeying for position at the motorway toll booths *(Péage)* below seems a world away.

On meeting the U-bend of a track, turn left uphill (sign: 'Fort de la Revère'). You emerge at a large doline (basin) and the **Maison de la Nature** (**1h25min**), with an interesting little museum, well-landscaped gardens, and picnic tables. Before continuing towards Eze, walk downhill to the coastal overlook (with benches) and follow the **corniche track** for short way. After five minutes, just before the **first tunnel**, a ***sentier botanique*** (with a *table d'orientation*) turns sharply up to the left — a possible detour. Continue through the **second tunnel** (**1h40min**), to take in the superb coastal panorama.

(***For the Alternative walk,*** continue along this track, eventually forking left to a water tank on the **Cime de la Forna**. Fork left again, to descend a stony path back to the reservoirs, and from there retrace your steps to La Turbie. See violet line on the map.)

La Trophée des Alpes: built in 6BC from almost pure-white local stone, it originally rose to 50m/165ft. It stood on the Via Julia Augusta, in commemoration of Roman victories over 44 different Alpine tribes. Sacked at the end of the Roman Empire, the trophy was mined by the troops of Louis XIV and then used as a quarry (La Turbie's church incorporates some of its stone); a museum relates its skilful restoration in the early 1900s.

To continue the main walk, retrace your steps to the Maison de la Nature and start walking up the road towards the **Fort de la Revère**. But after less than 100m/yds, turn left down a footpath (sign: 'Eze Village'). This pretty path descends through tall grass above some luxurious villas. On coming to a concrete drive, follow it downhill to the right. Keep right, downhill, at further junctions, until you meet the **Grande Corniche** again (**2h 05min**). Cross *carefully*, turn right for 20m/yds, then turn left down a lane, the **Chemin Serre de Forque**. The shade of pines is welcome here, but the descent is *very* steep. Keep straight down — by path, steps, or tar, until you meet the N7, the **Moyenne Corniche**, opposite the entrance to **Eze Village (2h 20min; bus shelter**, cafés). End the Shorter walk here, or take a break before, knees a-tremble, you begin the final descent.

The walk begins here at the pretty, arcaded *mairie* in La Turbie, where you cross over to the (closed) Hotel Napoléon.

Cross the road and head up into Eze, passing the **tourist office** on your right. Just past the **Fragonard** shop on your left, you will turn left down the **Chemin Frédéric Nietzche** (sign: 'Eze Mer'). But first join the crowds and walk on through this enchanting village — to visit the tropical gardens, church and White Pentitents' Chapel (just below the Nid d'Aigle restaurant).

Nietzche's wide old mule trail (he apparently climbed it every morning from his house on the coast) descends in gentle zigzags through a surprisingly wild valley (**Vallon du Duc**) above deeply-cut *calanques*. Eventually the path turns right, crosses a **col** (**2h50min**) and makes the final descent — with fine views over Cap Ferrat. When you meet the N98 (**Corniche Inférieure**) at **Eze-Bord-de-Mer**, turn right to the **bus stop**. The **railway station** and another **tourist office** are 400m/yds further along, on the south side of the road (**3h15min**).

Le Nid d'Aigle

Being such a tourist magnet, there are restaurants galore in Eze. Unless you just want an ice-cream, give the ones near the main road a miss and walk up to the very top of the village. Here you'll find the *very welcoming* Nid d'Aigle, a homely place with stone and wood décor, Provençal fabrics on the tables, and fantastic views over the village rooftops to the sea. In fine weather you can eat out on the walled terrace, under the shade of a venerable mulberry tree.

The Sauvage family have run the restaurant for 14 years under the guidance of Mme Marie; her daughter, Dominique is married to the head chef, Fabrice (but there are two other 'Fabrice' in the kitchen). We are always waited on by Aurélian, who feels part of the family, although he isn't.

On our last visit, Aurélian showed us the web site they were setting up (www.leniddaigle.fr), so we didn't bother to write down the whole list of specialities. But as we go to press with this second edition, the site still isn't showing the dishes, only photos of the restaurant. Keep trying!

The short (winter) menu shown here doesn't really do justice to their delicious food: the lamb fillets are served in their own juices, subtly flavoured with rosemary. The fish may have a sauce of tomatoes, basil, lemon, saffron, coriander and olive oil.

Should you be doing the Alternative walk and missing out Eze, try **Le Café de la Fontaine**. It's a short way to the *right* of the Hotel Napoléon (where the walk turns left), on the D2564, by the fountain. Open from 07.00, closed Mondays in winter; €-€€; ✆ 04 93 28 52 79. Their web site *is* working (www.hostelleriejerome.com/

The cosy interior at the Nid d'Aigle, just before lunch time. Everyone is still out on the walled terrace, enjoying the fine autumn weather.

LE NID D'AIGLE
1 Rue du Château ☎ 04 93 41 19 08
closed Wed and dinner time from Nov-Easter, then open daily for lunch and for dinner on Fri-Mon
€-€€

wide range of **drinks, sweets, snacks all day**

eight **entrees** — salads, *escargots*, charcuterie, *soupe au pistou*

three kinds of **fish**, depending on the season

meat: lamb, steak, rabbit (see photograph on page 79)

pancottas (large slices of bread with pizza-style toppings)

four kinds of **pasta** with five different sauces

pages/le-cafe-de-la-fontaine.cfm), so see what a superb lunch or dinner you could have for just 25 €! And you won't feel out of place in walking gear, despite the fact that it's owned by the very swish and expensive Hostellerie Jérôme (with two Michelin stars).

NEW YEAR'S DAY RABBIT

We worked up such an appetite when rabbit was on the menu in La Turbie at the start of the walk that we made this dish at our apart-hotel the following New Year's Day. We ordered a fresh rabbit in advance from the Buffa market —this is highly recommended, but you *can* buy packaged whole rabbits or rabbit pieces (legs or saddle) in all French supermarkets.

Caramelized rabbit with lemon *(lapin au caramel et citron)*

Preheat the oven to 190°C, 375°F, gas mark 5. Coat the rabbit pieces with the sugar. Melt the butter in a large frying pan, add the rabbit and cook gently until the sugar has caramelized. Then set the meat aside.

Add the lemon juice and a little stock to the pan and use a wooden spoon to deglaze (scrape any flavourful bits clinging to the pan into the liquid). Then set aside this mixture aside separately.

If you have a cast-iron casserole, the rest of the preparation can be done in it, but if you only have a pyrex casserole (as is usual in apart-hotels), continue by cleaning out the frying pan and using it again.

Heat the oil, add the *lardons,* and cook gently until fairly crispy, then set aside, leaving the oil and bacon fat in the pan. Put in the onion, carrots, and garlic and fry gently until softened. Add the liquefied cornflour, remaining stock, tomato purée, wine, lemon juice with deglazed pan bits, and the grated lemon rind. Using a wooden spoon, stir constantly until this comes to a boil. Then turn down and simmer until it reduces to a shiny glaze. Add salt and pepper, and the *herbes de provence,* stir, and turn off the heat.

recipes

eat

One winter Sunday when we set out, rabbit was the day's special at the up-market restaurant in the now-defunct Hotel Napoléon. It inspired us to create this recipe, which we often make at home. But since then, we've enjoyed superb rabbit at Le Nid d'Aigle. This photograph is of their rabbit dish, *not* ours.

Put the rabbit, lardons and liquid mixture into a casserole and stir to mix. The liquid should just cover the meat (if it does not, add more wine!).

Cover the casserole and place in the preheated oven for 50min to 1h. When it is cooked, the meat should be falling off the bone.

With a slotted spoon remove the rabbit pieces and other large bits and set aside on a preheated serving dish.

Simmer the remaining liquid if necessary, until it reduces. Add the port and cream and reheat *(but don't let it boil!).* Adjust the seasoning and pour the sauce over the rabbit.

Ingredients (for 4 people)

1.5 kg rabbit, jointed
75 g caster sugar
50 g butter
4 tbsp lemon juice
300 ml vegetable stock
1 large onion, finely chopped
2 tbsp olive oil
100 g diced rindless streaky bacon, unsmoked *(lardons nature)*
1 garlic clove, crushed
1 tbsp cornflour, liquefied in 1 tbsp cold lemon juice
2 tsp tomato purée
grated rind of one lemon
2 carrots, sliced
150 ml red wine
1 tsp *herbes de provence*
3 tbsp port
3 tbsp cream
salt and freshly ground pepper

The tangle of old cobbled lanes at Ste-Agnès, woven below arched passageways, evokes medieval times. But while this 'highest of Europe's coastal villages' has always been important strategically (the fort was the most southerly defence of the Maginot Line), no road was built until 1933. This walk follows an old mule trail.

st-agnès and castellar

WALK 7

Distance: 7km/4.3mi; 2h35min

Grade: easy-moderate ups and downs — about 500m/1640ft of descent overall and 270m/885ft of ascent (of which 200m is at the end of the walk). Red and white GR waymarking. *IGN map 3742 OT*

Equipment: see page 9; stout shoes, sun protection

Transport: 🚌 from Nice to Menton (every 15min); journey time 50min. Alight at Menton's bus station and change to 🚌 902 to Ste-Agnès (09.50 daily, also 11.30 Sat); journey time 25min. Return to Menton on 🚌 903 from Castellar (15.40 and 17.40 Mon-Sat); journey time 20min.

Refreshments en route: restaurants and/or cafés at Ste-Agnès (start), Monti (middle), Castellar (end)

Points of interest:

villages of Ste-Agnès and Castellar, including craft shops and artists' studios

old mule trails

The walk begins at the **Col St-Sébastien**, 200m/yds below **Ste-Agnès**, at the junction with the D22 to the Col de Gorbio. There's a **medieval chapel** here, a **fountain**, and a barrage of signposts. Follow the old cobbled footpath descending below the chapel, the GR51 (sign: 'La Virette, Monti, Castellar'.) In six minutes, when you have to go through an electrified wire fence, use the insulated handle to open the gate and close it behind you.

As you descend into the wilderness of the **Borrigo Valley**, it's hard to believe that you're just a short way inland from the busy coast. You pass a stand of cypresses that once gave welcome shade to travellers ascending to Ste-Agnès and descend to the grassy banks of the stream, a lovely place to while away an hour ... or three! When you come to the stream crossing, the horses from the enclosure above may already be slaking their thirst. After a short rise up the far bank, another electrified fence sees you out of the horses' pastures. Look ahead now to your destination — the honey-hued buildings of Castellar, strung along a ridge.

You pass through a rock chaos in a grove of trees (obviously a popular, shady picnic spot) and then another rock chaos. Beyond a small stream bed, you rise to the ruined hamlet of **La Virette** (**35min**).

Descending steeply from the ruins, watch carefully for the GR 'change of direction' sign and turn *sharp left* downhill, *ignoring* any yellow waymarks. Cross another stream (in the **Ravin de Merthea**) and rise quite steeply, past a short narrow section with a drop to the right. As you head southeast on the far side of this ravine, look back to Ste-Agnès, where its strategic position on the rocky escarpment is evident. Your eye will also be drawn to the motorway below, and the Monastère de l'Annonciade at Menton.

The old stone-paved mule trail up to Castellar

Dip into yet another little gully, the **Ravin de Cabrolles** — a cool glen in summer, where ivy twines round the trees. Having climbed up the far side, a wide cobbled trail comes in from the left behind you; here you look straight

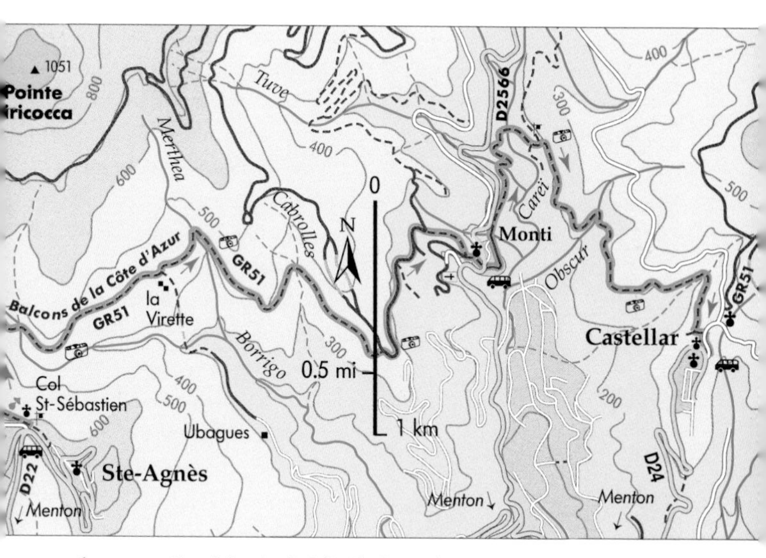

down on Cap Martin (Walk 8). Straight away you come onto a bulldozed track: *follow the GR waymarks carefully* on the next stretch, as there are several eroded bulldozed tracks in this area. Basically you should be contouring, descending slightly, until a fork to the right takes you back onto a path.

On coming to a concrete-surfaced T-junction, turn right. Steps take you down to the **church** at **Monti** (**1h35min**). Cross over to the **Auberge Pierrot Pierrette** (see page 85), then turn sharp left just past the **bus shelter**; your concrete path continues just behind it (although it looks as if you are walking straight into someone's property!). Descend towards an industrial area but, just before reaching it, go straight ahead along a track (just

Like St-Agnès, Castellar is home to many artists and artisans. In this Italinate village, the *trompe l'oeil* influence is pervasive.

past a huge pylon). Walk to the left of a glass and breeze-block wall (Pierrot Pierette's private swimming pool).

Now you start to round the final large valley before Castellar, the **Torrent Careï**. Immediately after crossing a stream, keep left uphill at a Y-fork. Then, just as you start to rise on concrete steps, fork right on a path, through a pretty, wooded section. Cross another stream and, on meeting a concrete road, follow it uphill to the left. But a short way up, fork sharp right (sign: 'Castellar'). This takes you down a concrete path.

Cross the main stream and, at a fork, keep left uphill (sign: 'Castellar 1h'). But fork right just 15 paces along. The path climbs in easy zigzags, sometimes through vineyards, and with an excellent view to Castellar on the approach. On coming to a crossing concrete lane, turn left uphill to a **chapel** on the **Avenue St-Anton** in **Castellar** (**2h35min**). Follow the road uphill to the right, then take steps up right, into the heart of the village. At the top of the steps there is an **iron cross**; opposite is the **bus stop**.

There are several restaurants in **Ste-Agnès**, among them **Le Righi** and the **Saint-Yves**. At **Castellar** the **Hôtel des Alpes** (1 Place Clemenceau, ✆ 04 93 35 82 83; €-€€) offers regional and traditional cooking — dishes like home-made terrine of pork and rabbit with herbs. We've yet to find 'the' place to have dinner at **Menton** (from where there are frequent buses till late at night). A recent meal at the recommended **L'Occitan** (behind the market; €; closed Mon; ✆ 04 93 41 67 76) was disappointing, with indifferent service and poorly-prepared, cold vegetables. If you're in a hurry, **Le Terminus** (€; ✆ 04 92 10 49 80), just by the railway station, specialises in regional dishes and is amazingly cheap.

Our favourite place to stop is **Pierrot Pierrette** at **Monti** (with rooms). If you have a three-course meal, it will be quite expensive (menus at 27 €, 39 €), so *linger* over a long lunch and take bus 910 back to Menton (daily at 17.14). We just have a *suberb* entree or main course with a carafe of the excellent house wine (€-€€), then continue our walk.

AUBERGE PIERROT PIERETTE
Place de l'Eglise ✆ 04 93 35 79 76
closed Mon and 1/12-15/1 €-€€€

specialities include *foie gras* pan fried with apples, pigeon with *foie gras*, red mullet fillets Provençe-style, mini-*bouillabaisse*

wide selection of **entrees**, including *escargots*, frogs' legs, various **pastas**

beautifully presented **fish**, like John Dory or the red mullet shown here

meats — not only the usual lamb and steaks, but rabbit and kidneys *(rognons de veau)*

elaborate **sweets**, good **cheese** board, gorgeous **house white wine**

Menton at Christmas, on the Avenue de Sospel, just south of the bus station. The vi
north towards Castellar and Sospel, further north, are clear as a bell. Some trees
painted with 'snow', others hanging heavy with oranges. But Menton is chiefly known
lemons, with a lemon festival in February. Menton's lemon pie is a must!

A LEMON FESTIVAL TARTE

Menton lemon pie *(tarte aux citrons de Menton)*

Prepare shortcrust pastry and leave in the fridge for 30min-1h. Preheat the oven to 190°C, 375°F, gas mark 5, with a baking tray on the middle shelf. Roll out the pastry and carefully place in an 22 cm pie tin, then bake for 25 minutes, until it is golden and crispy.

While the pastry is baking, prepare the filling. Gently warm the milk. Mix together the egg yolks, sugar and flour.

Using a wooden spoon, gradually stir the milk into the egg mixture. Then add the lemon juice and grated peel. Thicken this mixture in a double boiler (bain-marie) or a bowl placed over a saucepan of boiling water.

Cool the filling. Whisk the egg whites with a little sugar until peaks form and the mixture begins to glisten. Spread the filling over the pre-cooked pastry and cover with the egg whites. Return to the oven and bake until the egg whites become golden (about 10min).

Ingredients (for 8 servings)

- shortcrust pastry, made in advance, or ready-made
- 4 large eggs, separated
- 80 g caster sugar
- 2 tbsp plain flour
- 500 ml milk
- juice and grated peel of 3 lemons

Cap Martin is to Menton what Cap Ferrat is to Nice – an exclusive enclave of the seriously wealthy. But their coastal paths are accessible to everyone, so for a while you can be 'master of all you survey' – the princely views are free.

8 cap martin WALK

Start the walk at the **railway station** for **Roquebrune-Cap-Martin**. Cross the bridge over the railway, then turn left and make your way over to the coastal path, **'Le Corbusier'** (**5min**). Trailing fine views back to Monaco, you pass several spurs down to jumping-off points where you could swim but, remember,

Distance: 5km/3mi; 1h45min

Grade: easy, with gentle ups and downs, mostly on a concrete walkway. *IGN map 3742 OT*

Equipment: see page 9; bathing things, sun protection

Transport: 🚆 to Roquebrune-Cap-Martin (hourly from Nice station; see www.ter-sncf.com) or 🚌 100 to Roquebrune-Cap-Martin (the bus stop on the N7 is 80m/260ft above the station, so allow extra time for the descent/ascent). Same transport to return. Or 🚗

Refreshments: café at the railway station, restaurants on the coast from Cap Martin to Menton

Points of interest: coastal path and views

Note: You could begin by visiting the hill village of **Roquebrune**, with the oldest feudal castle in France (🚌 113 from Menton at 08.30, 10.50 Mon-Sat), stay for lunch, and then take steps (the 'Escalier Saft') 250m/820ft down to the coast, to begin the walk.

The coastal walkway

the sea is at least 10m/30ft deep here. (The path is named in memory of the architect, who *drowned* while swimming off these rocks.)

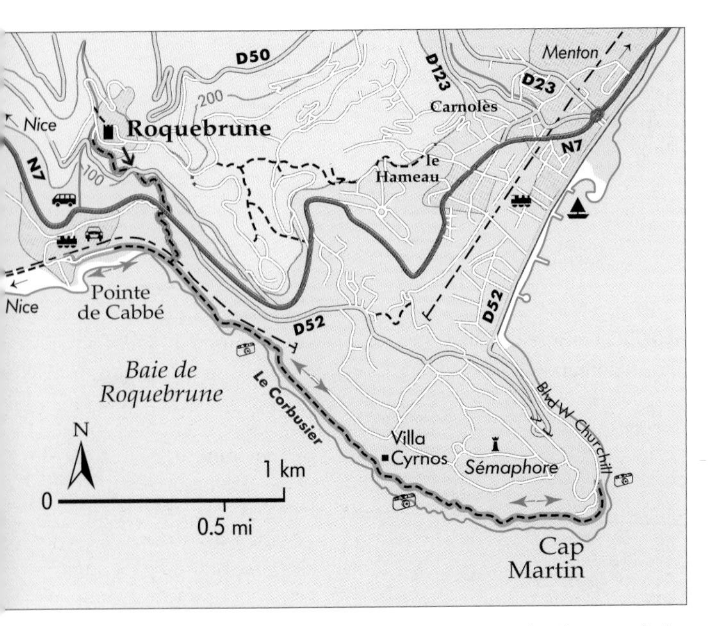

You pass below the **Villa Cyrnos**, once the home of the Empress Eugénie, where Winston Churchill came to paint and dine. Finally you skirt the grounds of the exclusive Résidence du Cap hotel, then round the tip of the cape, with fine views over to Menton.

The path ends at the **Boulevard Winston Churchill (55min)**. Retrace your steps from here. With views focussing on Monaco, Cap Ferrat, the Tête de Chien, La Turbie and the inland hill village of Roquebrune, return to the **Roquebrune-Cap-Martin railway station (1h45min)**.

Since we usually walk here in winter, when the coast east of Cap Martin tends to be quiet (except for the February festivals), we go back to Nice in the evening. But if you start the walk at **Roquebrune**, you may want to have lunch there. For a light meal, try **La Grotte**, a bar-café on the esplanade at the foot of the village serving everything from snacks to hearty fare (3 Place des Deux Frères, ✆ 04 93 35 00 04, closed Wed and last week of Oct; €).

La Canne à Sucre

When our base restaurant is closed, we *have* to experiment, even choosing one of those Promenade open-fronted restaurants we usually avoid. What to do when one of you wants 'unusual' fish and the other 'just' a pizza? *Very* few restaurants offer both.

La Canne à Sucre not only has a huge menu, but the food is delicious and the service superb. On our first visit, John had exquisite grilled turbot, filleted (perfectly) for him at the table, with boiled potatoes and a few perfectly-formed veg. Not expecting miracles, Pat (who *hates* thick crust) ordered the simplest pizza on the menu — just tomatoes and cheese. It came on a base almost as thin and crackling as a potato crisp. We've been back quite a few times, with the same results, and were pleased to see the delightful piano bar they opened in 2007 (separate entrance on the corner of rue du Congrès and the Promenade).

LA CANNE A SUCRE
11 Promenade des Anglais
✆ 04 93 87 19 35
daily, all year, 08.00-22.00 €-€€€

huge and varied menu, which can be downloaded at www.nice-restaurant.com (English version)

entrées from onion soup to terrine de *foie gras* with sauterne; **salads**; many different kinds of fresh **fish and seafood**; **meat**; freshly made **pastas** and **pizzas**; **local dishes** like ***daube*** (see page 102); large array of **sweets**

TWO WAYS WITH FISH FILLETS

Inspired by John's meal at La Canne à Sucre, we found some turbot recipes ... but no turbot. These recipes work well with halibut, John Dory, orange roughy, sole or dorade, more easily found in the UK.

Turbot (or halibut, etc) in sparkling wine (*turbot au champagne*)

Ingredients (for 4 people)

4 large fish fillets, ideally turbot or halibut
50 g butter
1 medium onion, finely chopped
1 bunch watercress (keep a bit to garnish, remove stalks and chop the rest)
300 ml warm milk
salt and freshly ground black pepper
1 bay leaf, torn in 4 pieces
300 ml sparkling white wine

Preheat the oven to 190°C, 375°F, gas mark 5. Unless you have an electric blender, take the time to chop the onions and cress *very finely*. Melt the butter in a pan and fry the onion gently until soft. Add the chopped watercress and fry for a further 2 minutes, stirring constantly. Stir in the warm milk; add salt and pepper to taste. Bring to the boil, then lower the heat, cover, and simmer for 15 minutes. Then rest at room temperature.

While the sauce is simmering, lay the fillets (flat, not overlapping) in a large, well-buttered baking tray. (If all you have in rented accommodation is a roasting pan, first line it with foil.) Season the fish to taste and place a bit of bay leaf on each. Pour over the wine, then cover with buttered foil and bake according to the thickness of the fish (allow 8min for each 10 mm thickness). Remove the fish with a slotted spatula, discard the bay leaves, and set aside on a warm platter. Cover with foil; keep hot.

Ideally one now purées the wine from the fish with the milk/cress/onion sauce in a blender, but this is not mandatory. Instead, add the warm wine to the sauce a little at a time and, stirring constantly, reduce over a high heat. Adjust the seasoning and pour over the fish. Garnish with the watercress sprigs.

Turbot (or halibut, etc) *à la provençale*

Quantities and cooking times/temperatures for this recipe (from La Mère Besson) are much the same as opposite. Make (or buy) a *court bouillon* (see page 69) using a bouquet garni, some minced shallots, lemon juice, salt, pepper and white wine. Set aside and chill.

Place the fish in the liquid in an oven dish (remember, if you overlap the fish, the cooking time will be longer). Bake according to thickness, or until it flakes easily. Then remove and keep warm.

Strain the cooking liquid and reduce over a high heat in a heavy pan. At the same time sauté quickly a handful of minced button mushrooms and add these to the reduced sauce. Whisk together one egg yolk with a tablespoon of cream, and whisk it into the sauce to thicken. Pour around the fish. Garnish with the tomatoes *(tightly clustered)* and parsley.

Ingredients (for 4 people)

- 4 large fish fillets (ideally turbot, halibut, John Dory)
- *court bouillon* (see page 69 and ingredients above)
- 1 egg yolk
- 1 tbsp cream
- 100 g button mushrooms, minced
- salt and pepper to taste
- 2 tomatoes, skinned, deseeded and diced into 1 cm cubes
- some fresh parsley, chopped

No trip to the south of France is complete without a journey on the delightful Train des Pignes (perhaps named for the pine cones the locals collected on Sundays to take back home; theories vary). Not only is the journey a splendid way to see the mountains, but a very pleasant way to get to Walks 9 and 10.

1 train des pignes EXCURSION

After the County of Nice was returned to France in 1860, there was great interest in linking the newly re-won Alps with the coast. Every valley wanted its own train. One of the surprisingly numerous projects to get off the drawing board, despite obstacles of terrain and financing, was the line built from Nice to Digne between 1890 and 1912 — spanning 150km with 16 viaducts, 17 bridges, and 25 tunnels, one of them 3km long! Some other railways built at this time, at enormous cost and effort, have not survived: the viaducts on the line to Barcelonnette are now drowned beneath the Lac de Serre-Ponçon; the Caramel Viaduct (which can be seen as you rise up the old mule trail to Castellar during Walk 7) is the sad remains of the route from Menton to Sospel.

This is a 'friendly' train; it

Departures: from Nice daily at 06.25 and 08.50; back from Digne at 17.30. Journey time 3h15min. There are other departures from both ends of the line, but the trains do not cover the entire route: see timetables at www.trainprovence.com: click on 'Nice > Digne', then on 'Horaires'. The operators (Chemins de Fer de Provence) also run a touristic steam train between Puget-Théniers and Annot. Note: departures are from 3 on the plan, *not* from the main SNCF railway station.

Hints: The little train is very comfortable, with large padded seats and 'sightseeing-size' windows. Travelling north, sit on the right-hand side; travelling south, sit on the left. *Don't* make the mistake of sitting in the front row — the guard may monopolise the front windows! Take a map, to pinpoint all the sights en route. The train stops for a good five minutes at Annot, where those 'in the know' alight to have a cup of coffee at the pleasant station restaurant.

If you enjoy walking from the train, keep an eye open in Nice bookshops (or the Chemin de Fer station) for books or leaflets describing other walks you can do from the train. They appear, go out of print, and then often reappear in the shops.

ALPES-DE-HAUTE-PROVENCE
Allos, Colmars
St-Martin-d'Entraunes
Sisteron
Thorame-Haute
Verdon
Digne-les-Bains
Font-Gaillarde
Thorame-Haute-Gare
Méailles
N85
Châteauredon
Bléone
les Mées
St-André-les-Alpes
10
Grès d'Annot
Annot
N85
Train des Pignes
Barrême
Moriez
N202
Entreva
Col de Toutes Aures
Lac de Castillon
Demandolx
Moustiers-Ste-Marie
Castellane
St Auban
Valensole
Point Sublime
N85
Route Napoléon
le Logis
Seranon
la Palud
Riez
Aix
Lac de Ste-Croix
Corniche Sublime
Grand Canyon du Verdon
Comps
Mons
Baudinard
Verdon
Plan de Canjuers
Bargemon
Montmeyan
Fayence
Aups
VAR
Callas
Tavernes
Tourtour
Bagnols
Toulon
Barjols
Salernes
Draguignan

Parc National du Mercantour
Madone de Fenestre
le Boréon
Tende
Beuil
Valberg
St-Sauveur-sur-Tinée
St-Martin-Vésubie
Vallon de la Gordolasque
11
Belvédère
12
Gorges du Cians
Tinée
la Bollène
Col de Turini
Puget-Théniers
9
Touët
N202
Madone d'Utelle
Utelle
Vésubie
Train des Pignes
Var
ITALIA
Bonson
Plan-du-Var
Sospel
Sigale
Roquesteron
Aiglun
7
Castellar
Esteron
ALPES-MARITIMES
Peillon
Aspremont
3
Ventimiglia
Coursegoules
N7
A8/E80
Menton
Carros
2
8
la Turbie
Roquebrune
Cap Martin
Vence
6
Monte Carlo
N202
Var
Eze
Gourdon
Beaulieu
le Bar
1
4
Cagnes
Cap Ferrat
St-Vallier
Grasse
Cézaire
Nice
N
N85
N98
Antibes
Lac de St-Cassien
N7
Juan-les-Pins
A8/E80
Cannes
Cap d'Antibes
la Napoule
5
Théoule
Esterel

Entrevaux — a magical village you can visit with the Train des Pignes

will stop to drop off or pick up walkers virtually anywhere along the run. If you *do* manage to find a guide to walks along the route (in French), remember that the walks vary enormously in interest and difficulty and *should not be attempted without the relevant large-scale IGN map!*

Leaving Nice, the train moves like a tram through the city and into the suburbs. Soon it's hurtling along the wide basin of the **Var River**. At **Colomars** look up left, above the industrial spread of modern-day Carros beside the river, to Carros-Village and Le Broc perched on the hillside. At **St-Martin-du-Var**, the **Esteron Valley** comes in from the left. Beyond **Plan-du-Var**, don't miss the mouth of the **Vésubie Gorge**, seen through the Pont Durandy on the right. The perched village of **Bonson** rises on the left. Now you're in the **Defilé du Chaudan**, between the two carriageways of the N202, racing the motorists. Just beyond a tunnel look out right for the towering walls of the **Tinée Gorge**, backed by the mountains of the Mercantour. Small farmholdings introduce **Toüet-sur-Var**, huddled below a rock cliff. Then the most magnificent of all the gorges opens up — the **Cians Gorge** (Excursion 2 takes you up this gorge). Alight at **Puget-Théniers** for Walk 9, or continue past a 5km-long stretch of orchards and plane trees lining the way to **Entrevaux**, the fairy-tale village shown opposite.

Past the gap of the **Daluis Gorge**, watch for some high bluffs on the right: Walk 10 rounds a ledge almost at the very top (see photograph on page 112). At **Annot** notice the houses built into boulders like those shown on page 110 (the '**Grès d'Annot**') and the chaos of *grès* just as you leave, as well as the *robines* (see

The little train (shown here at Annot station) runs all year round. In winter it's equipped with a snow plough. The only time it stops is when there is one of the (fairly frequent) strikes!

page 107). Now the train hurtles through the rolling fields and orchards of the verdant **Vaïre Valley** to **Méailles**.

A 3km-long tunnel precedes **Thorame-Haute-Gare**. Still the little train tears along, shrugging off the fact that it has already climbed 1000m from Nice! The gorgeous **Verdon Valley** is followed to **St-André**. You have a fine view of the church and the **Lac de Castillon** as you leave — watch for paragliders here.

Following the **Asse de Moriez**, come to **Moriez**: just outside it there are interesting rock dykes. A 12th-century chapel rises on a hill outside **Barrême**, where a huge fir graces the station. Now the N85 *(***Route Napoléon***)* is just beside you on the right, and you skirt the **Forêt Domaniale des Trois Asses**, as you follow the Asse de Blieux via the **Clue de Chabrières** (on the left) to **Châteauredon**. From here the train curves north and crosses the wide **Bléone River**, before coming into **Digne**, below the Alpes de Haute-Provence. Out of the station, turn left to walk into the town (about 15 minutes).

We can't tell you anything about restaurants in Digne; we haven't gone that far for years. We either leave the train to walk from Annot (restaurants below) or Puget-Théniers (see page 108).

Or we just take the train to marvel at **Entrevaux**, where there's a hotel-restaurant just by the station: **Le Vauban** (☎ 04 93 05 42 40; closed Sun evenings and all day Mon from Nov-Easter; menus at 16 € and 26 €). The décor is warm and homely; the menu includes seasonal dishes of *daube,* wild boar, or even sweetbreads — as well as *secca* (dried salt beef with olive oil and lemon juice, a local speciality). The terrace (shown right) has fine views towards the Entrevaux setting. If you visit on a day when they are closed, ask at the tourist office (☎ 04 93 05 46 73) about other restaurants when you pick up some leaflets about this magnificent site.

If you go on to **Annot** for Walk 10, there are several hotels with restaurants, at least one of which will be open out of season. Ask at the tourist office. We show *approximate* closing dates. Out of the station, take the road into the village. You pass **L'Avenue**, on the left (listed in the Michelin Red Guide; ☎ 04 92 83 22 07, closed 04/11-Easter). A few steps further along, just to the *left* on the main road, is the restaurant **Le Versus** (☎ 04 92 83 31 80; menu from € 12,50; terrace; closed Tue/Wed and 15/12-15/02). Turning *right* on the main road you come to the main square with the hotel **Le Parc** (☎ 04 92 83 20 03, closed 01/10-30/04), as well as the tourist office (on the left). A short way straight ahead is the charming hotel-restaurant **La Cigale** (☎ 04 92 83 20 24, closed Jan/Feb), but the menu can be limited out of season: the only main course on the day we visited was squid stew!

DAUBE A LA PROVENÇALE

In case you missed *daube* at Le Vauban in Entrevaux, try this easy recipe. *Note:* not all recipes call for wine vinegar, so only add this if you want the extra, slightly sour 'kick. Cut the meat into 3-4 cm cubes and marinate overnight with one onion, one carrot, the cloves, thyme and bay, salt, pepper, wine (and vinegar).

Preheat the oven to 180°C, 350°F, gas mark 4. Remove the meat from the marinade. Brown it bit by bit on all sides in a heavy-bottomed pan, transfering each lot of meat to a heavy casserole. Then fry the *lardons* and, when they are browned, add the garlic, carrots and onions. Swish all this around, then add to the casserole.

Add the stock, tomato purée, salt and pepper to the casserole. Cover and cook for 1h, then reduce the heat to 140°C, 300°F, gas mark 2 and cook for a further 4-5h, until the meat is meltingly tender. Pour the liquid into a separate pan, boil down to reduce to a shiny sauce, then pour back over the *daube*.

Ingredients (for 6 people)

1.5 kg lean beef, like shoulder *(paleron de boeuf)* or, even better, shin *(jarret de boeuf)*
100 g bacon bits *(lardons)*
3 medium onions, sliced
4 medium carrots, sliced
3 garlic cloves, crushed
50 ml wine vinegar (optional!)
4 level tbsp tomato purée
6 cloves
sprig fresh thyme, 2 bay leaves
salt and pepper to taste
500 ml red wine
200 ml beef or vegetable stock
olive oil or lard for browning

Caffé Promenade

We first found this place when we were staying up in the wilds of Puget-Théniers (see Walk 9) in cold, rainy weather. We took the Train des Pignes to Nice and just headed for the sea! The nearest bright lights turned out to be Caffé Promenade (28 on the plan), just a few doors from the tourist office.

Over the years we've tried a great many of their dishes. Our all-time favourites are their creamy **omelette and *frites*** and their delectable ***moules farcies*** (*tiny* tender mussels, grilled with a butter, parsley and garlic topping — a far cry from large, tough farmed mussels). *Warning:* the portions are huge; the staff are happy to let you share — just ask.

Either meal is delicious with their house rosé or Normandy cider: sweet *(doux)* or dry *(brut)*. Note that it is far more economical to order one *large* bottle of cider than to keep topping up.

CAFFE PROMENADE
3 Promenade des Anglais
(04 93 82 54 55
all year from 07.00-02.00 €-€€

economical **full English breakfast** — or continental — from 07.00

sandwiches of all kinds; **omelettes**, **salads** (including smoked salmon, chicken), ***moules frites***

several **pasta** dishes

steaks with golden *pommes frites* and side salad

ice-creams, **sweet trolley**, **very wide selection of teas**

This walk is a good introduction to the *robines* of Haute-Provence. Ranging in colour from off-white to black, they have an austere beauty. It also affords superb long-range views along the orchard valley of the Var, to say nothing of the opportunity to pick up local goodies at the superb tourist office by the station.

9 above puget-théniers WALK

Distance: 4.5km/2.8mi; 2h

Grade: moderate climb/descent of 330m/1100ft, but you must be sure-footed and have a head for heights. Avoid the walk in mist, strong winds and wet weather. Some of the paths cross *robines* (see next page), where *care is needed.* Yellow PR way-marking. *IGN map 3641 OT*

Equipment: see page 9; walking stick(s), sun protection

Transport: 🚂 to Puget-Théniers (Train des Pignes; departs Nice 06.25, 08.50, 12.55 daily from 3 on the plan); journey time 1h25min. Returns at 16.28, 19.36. Or 🚗: park at Puget-Théniers railway station.

Refreshments: cafés and restaurants at Puget-Théniers; none en route

Points of interest:

Puget-Théniers (Maillol statue, Romanesque church, castle site)

robines (see caption on page 107)

steam train to Annot on Sundays in summer (enquire at the station)

Start out from the **railway station** at **Puget-Théniers**. Walk into the village centre, then take steps at the right of the **post office** up to **Rue de la Redoule** and follow it to the **cemetery** (**15min**). From walkers' signpost 174 follow a path uphill, cross the road to the cemetery, and continue to the left of the telephone exchange (with the word 'judo' on the wall!). Keep right at a fork, then *left uphill* at the next fork (where a stronger path goes straight ahead). You join a fire-fighting road, which quickly becomes a track. Before the track makes a U-bend, be sure to *turn back sharp left* uphill on the waymarked route — a centuries-old trail. Climbing in zigzags, you enjoy fine views over Puget-Théniers and can trace the Var Valley from Utelle in the east to the castle at Entrevaux in the west. Reaching a **crest**, walk *(carefully)* along the very top of the *robines* pouring down into the **Ravin du Planet** on your right.

Before long, the path moves away from the edge and heads

The knife-sharp Castagnet Cliffs above Puget-Théniers

west, leaving a little ruined house up above to the right. From a **pass** (**1h**) you look ahead into the Roudoule Valley, backed by the Crête d'Aurafort. As the walk continues uphill in tight zigzags, be sure to locate your waymarks. The **Roccia d'Abeilla** (**1h15min**) marks the top of the climb: from here there is a magnificent view east along the Var. The 'Bee's Rock' is a natural fortress, from where *robines* pour down into the Ravin du Planet. Walk on to signpost 173 and, at the fork, keep straight ahead, to the ruined **Bergerie de Lava** (**1h20min**), where you can take a break on the grassy slopes.

The onward walk starts from the back of the *bergerie* and descends to the **Roudoule Valley**, with views to the Crête d'Aurafort, the Castagnet Cliffs and the roofs of Puget-Théniers. This narrow path is especially beautiful in autumn, when wine-red Venetian sumac and gold grass contrast with the dark shiny leaves of the holm oaks. Here again, *care is needed* on the *robines.* Finally the path crosses a very narrow ridge between two *robines* — this only lasts for 12m/yds, but is potentially dangerous on a windy day — and amazingly, this is when you return to 'civilisation' and are just above a house!

Robines — limey-clay slopes prone to erosion, are encountered on this walk and Walk 10 from Annot.

Join the drive to the house and, where it curves to the right, turn sharp left on a cart track. When this track turns towards a house, continue down a rough, grassy trail, making for the cemetery and telephone exchange. As you approach a wooden gate, turn sharp right down a footpath. Cross a gully on a **wooden footbridge** and come to the **Rue de la Roudoule** (and signpost 175; **1h50min**). Turn left, follow the road down to sign 174, and head back to **Puget-Théniers station** (**2h**). Before leaving, take time to visit the splendid tourist office next door! Not only are there leaflets, maps and books, but it is also a 'Maison du Pays' — a 'supermarket' of local produce!

L'Oustalet

This restaurant, next to the station at Puget-Théniers, might go unnoticed if you make straight for the centre (it's housed in the old station *buffet*). *Don't* miss it! It's a *very* popular, excellent restaurant specialising in local dishes. We drive up from Nice or come by train just for lunch. They are open almost all year. It's very cosy in winter, but in fine weather we like to watch the comings and goings of the Train de Pignes or the steam train, so we sit beside the railway line, out on the terrace (just behind the Virginia creeper in the photo).

Out of season, Puget centre can be rather a 'ghost town'. If L'Oustalet isn't open, either the **Hôtel Alizé** (opposite the station; ☎ 04 93 05 06 20) or the **Hotel Laugier** (in the pretty plane-shaded square behind the Maillol statue (☎ 04 93 05 01 00) should be; ask at the tourist office.

L'OUSTALET
by the station ☎ 04 93 05 04 11
closed Sun, Thu dinner and 1st week Apr €-€€ (menus at 10 €, 15 €, 18 €; gourmet menu at 21 €)
opens 09.00; last lunch orders 15.00

huge, sophisticated selection, from

light meals: sandwiches, omelettes, *secca* (the Entrevaux speciality mentioned on page 101), and 8 kinds of *bruschetta*

fresh pastas; 10 different sauces

fish including locally-caught trout, sea bass, sole

meat from duck to veal, sweetbreads, goulash of wild boar, *daube*, steaks with varied sauces

The Puget-Théniers tourist office/ 'Maison du Pays' is a treasure-trove of home-made local delicacies. You can buy whole prepared meals here in glass Kilner jars, and rest assured that there are *no additives or preservatives.* Here's one of the dishes we bought that was fairly easy to duplicate at home.

Mutton (or lamb) stew with chestnuts *(Navarin de mouton aux châtaignes)*

Ingredients (for 4 people)

- 800 g boneless mutton or lamb, cubed
- 100 g unsmoked bacon bits *(lardons natur)*
- 400 g haricot beans
- 100 g prepared chestnuts
- 200 ml red wine
- 200 ml stock
- 2 garlic cloves, crushed
- 1 tbsp tomato paste
- 1 tbsp olive oil
- 2 tbsp brandy
- 1 tsp *herbes de Provence*
- 1 bay leaf, in pieces
- salt and pepper

Brown the bacon bits in the olive oil, then add the garlic and cook for one minute. Set aside. In the same pan, brown the meat on all sides. Return all the meat to the pan, add the brandy and flame it, to burn off the alcohol. Then add the wine and bring just to the boil.

Transfer the meat/wine to a casserole, stir in the stock, beans, chestnuts, tomato puree, herbs, bay leaf, and salt and pepper to taste. Cook in a slow oven (160°C, 325°F, gas mark 4) for 2h30min. (If you prefer your beans and chestnuts more *'al dente'*, stir them in for just the last hour of cooking.)

Like all stews, this tastes better when reheated (at 200°C, 400°F, gas mark 6) for 35 minutes.

10

This magnificent walk, beautifully shaded by oaks and chestnuts, takes you through a chaos of towering eroded sandstone boulders and rock arches, the Grès d'Annot. Midway through the hike you skirt a cliff-face below massive rock 'totem-poles', high above the confluence of the Vaïre and Coulomp at Les Scaffarels.

grès d'annot

WALK

Distance: 5km/3mi; 2h15min

Grade: moderate climb/descent of 330m/1100ft, but you must be sure-footed on the *robines* (see photograph on page 107). Avoid the walk in mist or wet weather. Yellow PR waymarking. *IGN map 3541 OT*

Equipment: see page 9; walking stick(s), sun protection

Transport: 🚂 to Annot (Train des Pignes; departs Nice 06.25, 08.50, 12.55 daily from 3 on the plan); journey time 2h. Returns at 16.02, 19.10. Or 🚗: park at Annot station.

Refreshments: cafés, restaurants and hotels at Annot (see page 101)

Points of interest:
attractive old town of Annot
the *Grès d'Annot*
robines (see photo on page 107)
steam train to Puget-Théniers on Sundays in summer (enquire at the station)

Start out at the **railway station** at **Annot**: head downhill towards the village, then turn right and walk through a **tunnel** under the railway (sign: 'Circuit des Grès d'Annot, Chambre du Roi'). Then turn right on a stony track, passing the octagonal water tower for the old steam trains. Keep along to the last railway building (noticing the house up to the left, built into the first of the *grès* en route), where the tracks disappear into a shed (sign: 'Annot, Escalade sur les Grès'). Just past the sign, meet a fork and go left, climbing slightly.

When you are directly above the turntable for the old steam locomotives, be sure to turn left in the first zigzag of this **stone-laid mule trail** (**10min**). Climb into the rock chaos, where climbers have inscribed mythological names on the sandstone boulders. Paths thread out in all directions; *keep careful watch for the yellow waymarks.* If in doubt, whenever possible follow paths running parallel with the Vaïre Valley on the right (climbing southwest); don't head too far left. Beyond the chaos you

Rock 'totem poles' above the confluence of the Vaïre and Couloump

should find yourself on the stone-laid trail again (**30min**), soon crossing some clay slopes *(robines)* shored up with logs. Five minutes later more shored-up *robines* are crossed and there is a fine view to terracing on the far side of the Vaïre.

At a crossing of paths (**50min**), climb up to the right (sign: '**Chambre du Roi**'). In the shade of beautiful chestnuts you reach the narrow defile shown on page 110. As you start into it, look right: 'entree' is written on a stone. If you're slim enough, and not claustrophobic, squat down and crawl through this opening, into the three huge rock 'rooms', illuminated by a small gap high above. Then return and continue through the towering, shady defile. At the end of the passage you come to a **clearing** with a fireplace and boulder-benches — a lovely rest spot.

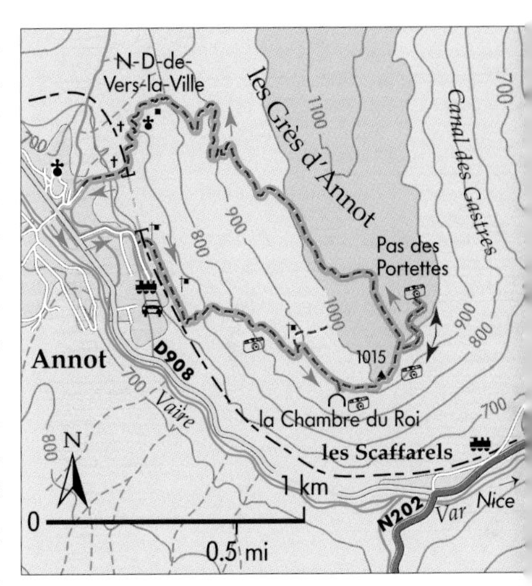

The path continues up to the cliff-edge above the confluence of roads and streams at Les Scaffarels, from where a fabulous 'balcony' path (amply wide, but watch your footing and *take special care* on windy days) carries you east in the setting shown opposite (**1h05min**). Once round the bluff, there are more breathtaking views over the apron of emerald cultivation skirting the Var. You now head inland through once-cultivated chestnut groves, which are losing ground to the faster-growing pines. (Soon a signposted path on the right indicates a possible detour north-northeast to a magnificent viewpoint over the Coulomp Valley. It's 15 minutes up and 10 minutes back down; *not* included in our times; *take care; the drops to the southeast are sheer!*)

The main path climbs gently over bedrock and then through a mossy glen, full of ferns and tall trees embraced by ivy. You pass to the right of a ruined **stone shelter** (**1h20min**) built below an overhang of rock, with a venerable chestnut in front. Now the path climbs quickly to the **Pas des Portettes**, the highest point of the walk. Turn left downhill here, passing under a high rock arch. As you descend into another rock chaos, enjoy the lovely play of light and shade, as the sun streams through the magnificent chestnuts onto the moss-covered boulders. Once in a while, the path climbs *very slightly* before descending again, but *be sure not to climb too far up to the right.*

Some seven-eight minutes below the pass, watch for your turn-off: you must go *sharp left* downhill. (If you find yourself walking north above Annot, you've gone too far.) Further downhill, several springs gush out over the path. which can be very wet at times, but it's pleasant to walk accompanied by the sound of running water.

You pass a building on the left dated 1672 and two minutes later come to the 12th-century chapel of **Notre-Dame-de-Vers-la-Ville** on the left (**1h55min**). Its wall-belfry is surmounted by a stone cross. From here a grassy stone-laid trail takes you downhill in zigzags, past the **14 Stations of the Cross**, each embellished with a naïve painting on glazed tiles. Cross the **railway line** and follow a lane between colourful gardens and fields. When you come into **Annot**, take a break for some refreshments, then head back on the main road, following 'gare' to return to the **station** (**2h15min**). Perhaps when you get back to Nice you'll have time to try the easy recipe opposite.

OSSO BUCCO NICE-STYLE

The Italian influence is everywhere evident in the cookery of Nice, no more so than this popular dish which gets its 'twist' from the addition of lemon (and, if you like, orange) zest. This is another recipe from La Mère Besson (see page 66).

Our recipe is a bit of a 'cheat's' osso bucco; we've used tinned (Italian plum) tomatoes. Heat the olive oil in a large, heavy-bottomed frying pan *with a lid*. Dust the meat with flour and brown lightly on both sides.

Turn down the heat. Add the onion, garlic, tomatoes and salt and pepper to taste. Pour over the wine and sprinkle with the zest.

Let all this cook slowly, covered, for 30min, then remove the lid and leave to simmer for another hour or more. While you are enjoying an apéritif or two, reminiscing about the Annot 'totem poles', the flour and marrow from the meat will merge with the wine to create a good sauce which should have reduced to perfection.

Serve with white rice or boiled potatoes.

Ingredients (for 4 people)

- 4 thick veal shins *(jarret de veau)* with marrow
- 1 small onion, finely chopped
- 2 garlic cloves, crushed
- 400 g tin chopped tomatoes
- 200 ml dry white wine
- grated rind of 2 lemons (and half an orange)
- flour to dust
- 4 tbsp olive oil
- salt and freshly ground pepper

2

This excursion — like the Train des Pignes — makes a wonderful day out, with a visit to the most spectacularly colourful gorge in the south of France. Beuil is a lovely walking base for most of the year, although the skiers take over in winter.

gorges du cians
EXCURSION

Ideally you will be sitting on the right-hand side of the bus as it pulls out of the *gare routière,* but make sure the windows are tinted, as you will be on the sunny side. The initial part of the trip follows the same route up the Var Valley as the Train des Pignes, so keep an eye out for all the sights mentioned on page 99.

Departures: 770 from Nice *(gare routière)* to/from Beuil; daily; journey time 2h25min. Alight at the tourist office. *From 15/6-15/9* out at 07.45, return at 17.00; *shoulder season* out at 08.45, return at 16.00; *skiing season* out at 07.15, return at 17.00.

Points of interest: The journey follows the same route as the Train des Pignes as far as the Cians Gorge: see notes on page 94. The highlight of this trip is the Cians Gorge, although the village of Beuil is very pretty, and Walk 11 is delightful.

Refreshments: cafés and hotel-restaurants at Beuil (see page 125)

Hints: Travelling north, sit on the right-hand side of the bus; travelling south, sit on the left.

After about an hour and a quarter, beyond Touët-sur-Var, the bus leaves the N202 and heads up the D28 through the honey-coloured chasms of the lower **Gorges du Cians** and below the small village of Rigaud. If you think this lower gorge is spectacular, wait till you see what lies ahead!

The first landmark of any note as you climb up this lonely stretch is pretty **Pra-d'Astier**, gateway to the upper gorge. Just after leaving the hamlet there is an abrupt transformation in the landscape: from honey, the rock colour changes to red — rust red, blood red, wine red. The contrast between the rock and the varying greens of the moss, ferns and trees is breathtaking.

Below is the rushing turquoise-to-emerald **Cians River**.

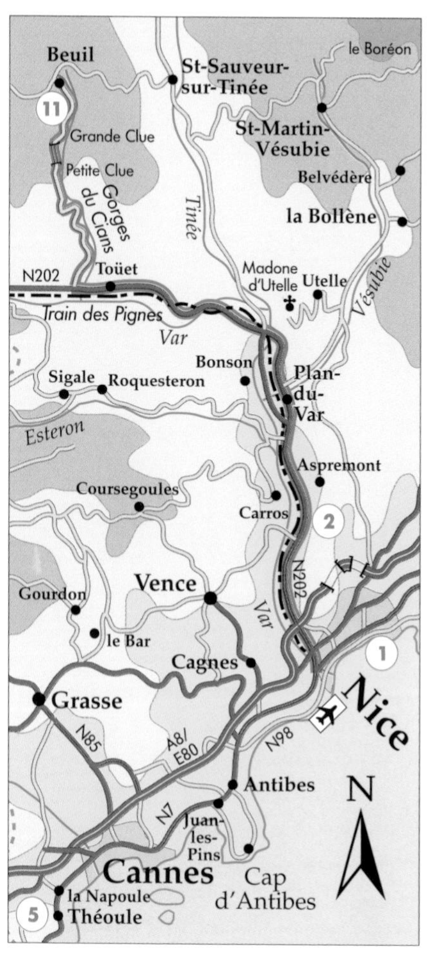

The river drops some 1600m/5250ft on its 22km descent from Beuil to the Var, and has left the towering red schist chasms in its wake.

Watch for signs alerting you to the **Petite and Grande Clues** — the most spectacular rifts. The D28 has been diverted through tunnels in both places, allowing sections of the curving old road to be converted into pedestrian walkways with spectacular views (see opposite).

When you get to **Beuil** you should have plenty of time to enjoy Walk 11 and take some refreshment in one of the cafés or hotels (see page 125).

Grande Clue in the upper Cians Gorge

11

While we try to avoid the eyesore development of most ski resorts, Beuil is an exception. Its setting is just stunning. There are several waymarked walks around this alpine village, but we're convinced that this circuit shows it off to best advantage, whatever the season.

above beuil

WALK

Distance: 8km/5mi; 2h45min

Grade: easy-moderate, with ascents/descents of 320m/1050ft overall. Little shade. Yellow PR way-marking; some short cross-country sections (no path) are marked with wooden sighting posts. *IGN map 3640 OT*

Equipment: see page 9; sun protection

Transport: 🚌 770 to Beuil (for details see page 117 and alight at the tourist office); or 🚗: park at the tourist office on the main road (D28).

Refreshments: cafés and hotel-restaurants at Beuil (see page 125); none en route

Points of interest:
alpine surroundings
Beuil village

Start out at the **tourist office** *(syndicat d'initiative)* on the main road (D28) in **Beuil**. Walk down the road (signposted to the Gorges du Cians). Some 300m/yds downhill, at walkers' signpost 52, fork right for 'Circuit de Bramafan'. The cinder track soon rises in zigzags, to a **shrine** on the right (signpost 53; **15min**). Continue straight ahead at this junction, ignoring the cart track to the right (your return route). Rising gently on the northeastern flanks of the **Plateau St-Jean**, you have fine views back to Beuil and down left into the **Cians Valley**, with the little St-Ginié chapel on the far bank.

At a Y-fork by some buildings (just past the shrine), keep left, on the main track. Beyond the hamlet of **Le Serre** (**25min**), you cross a stream. Beuil disappears from view, but Les Cluots (2106m/6907ft) in the southeast now attracts your attention: its summit is almost always snow-capped. **Rétouria** (**45min**) is another pretty little hamlet, with wooden-roofed stone houses and a good view down south towards the Cians Gorge.

At signpost 56 you come upon another handful of houses.

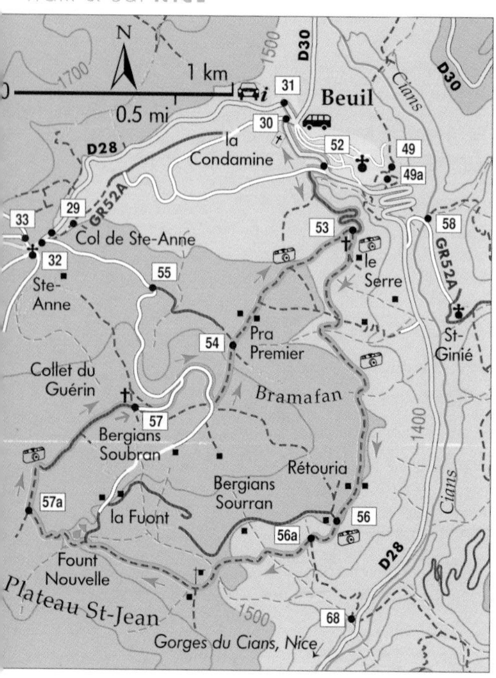

Go *left* here, for 'Cians', leaving the 'Bramafan' circuit and zig-zagging down towards the road in the Cians Gorge. When you reach signpost 56a (**55min**) some 60m/200ft downhill, turn right at the Y-fork (signposted towards 'Bergians Soubran'). This narrow and slightly overgrown (but well waymarked) path gently regains the height lost, as it rises to another group of houses and a wooden signpost: 'Itinéraire Pédestre'. Here you come to a Y-fork at a **barn** (**1h10min**). Both routes are waymarked, but *take the fork to the right of the barn.* Soon the path contours above fields, before coming into a patch of forest and then climbing gently through a stream bed wilderness.

At the **Fount Nouvelle** (**1h25min**) a cart track comes in from the right. Continue to the left of this well on a stony path, still rising up the stream bed. At a fork three minutes along, go right,

Rétouria and (right) the little shrine encountered some 15 minutes along

now climbing a bit more steeply. You pass to the left of a **concrete plinth** (take either path at the fork here). Then walk to the left of a wooden **sighting post**, making for the top of the ridge ahead, where the next sighting post is visible (no waymarks).

Having risen to a crossing track, follow it to the right, to signpost 57a (**1h42min**). From here head northeast towards 'Bergians Soubran', crossing a grassy **plateau**, with a 'top of the world' feeling. Giant thistles and thousands of sheep accompany you, as well as views north to the jagged peaks of the high Mercantour. The hamlet of La Fuont is below to the right.

Nearing **Bergians Soubran** you'll surely encounter goats, sheep, geese, hens, cows, horses, cats and dogs! At the **Collet du Guérin** (**1h55min**), where there is a **cross** on the left and signpost 57 on the right, keep straight ahead on a lane, passing a little turning circle on the right. At a T-junction, turn right on

All the little hamlets are beautifully kept; in autumn the wayside is decorated with blooms — seemingly just for the pleasure of walkers!

another lane, slightly uphill. The landscape is a blanket of golden grass interwoven with strands of firs and spruce.

Seven minutes from the col, after the lane has described a wide curve to the right, watch for a **sighting post** on the left and go left down a wide grassy path at the left edge of the woods. It drops straight down to a grassy track and signpost 54 (**2h10min**). Go half-right here, again following the 'Circuit de Bramafan' and passing between two cottages at **Pra Premier**. At a Y-fork, keep left downhill, straight towards Beuil. Soon the trail peters out, but just keep steeply downhill through the grassy field, towards a **metal pole** with a yellow flash. There is a beautiful view over the green valley of **La Condamine** and to Beuil.

More sighting posts lead you onto a cart track descending from the right. Follow this downhill to the left, to a huge **cairn**. Continue downhill at the left of the cairn, on an old trail, with the remains of stone walls on either side. This brings you back to the **shrine** first passed at the 15min-point (**2h25min**). Turn left and retrace your outward route to **Beuil** (**2h45min**).

There are a few hotel-restaurants in Beuil, as well as several bar-cafés. Closing dates are erratic; they open for the summer walking season and again for the winter skiing season, closing in spring and autumn. *Avoid November,* when you may go hungry! Phone ahead to the tourist office (✆ 04 93 02 32 58) to check what will be open.

HOTEL L'ESCAPADE
Beuil centre ✆ 04 93 02 31 27
closed 22/03-2/04 and 1/10-27/12
€-€€ (menus at 19 €, 24,50 €)

entrees include the beautifully presented ***assiette terroir***: platters of *terrine de foie de volaille* (chicken liver and mushroom) and sliced meats (either head-cheese or cured ham), trays of pickles and huge jars of wild *sanguin* mushrooms in olive oil are brought to your table; you help yourself

fish courses feature **local trout** in basil sauce

meats include steaks, *daube de boeuf* (thickened with corn starch), tripe sausage *(andouillette)*

wide range of **pastas** and ***petits farcis*** (see page 31) for a lighter meal

Our first choice would be the very friendly **Hotel l'Escapade** (on the main road to the church; mentioned in Michelin), which features regional cooking and has a pretty terrace. But there are others, including the **Relais de Bellevue** a little further along (✆ 04 93 02 30 04; closed 30/03-15/05 and 01/10-26/12).

If you are looking for a lighter meal, try the popular bar-crêperie **Tire-Bouchon** just past L'Escapade; it also features one 'plat du jour' (✆ 04 93 02 36 08; closed Nov; €).

CHESTNUTS AND CHARD

If you spend any time in the Mercantour National Park (Beuil is on the doorstep) no doubt you'll come across some menus using either chestnuts *(châtaignes)* or Swiss chard *(blettes)*. Here are a few popular recipes (all for four people). We've cheated by using prepared chestnuts — of course fresh would be better, if you have time!

Chestnut purée *(purée de châtaignes)*

Using packaged prepared chestnuts, simmer them very slowly with some salt and fennel leaves for 30 minutes. Then purée, adding milk (to the consistency of a bread sauce). Lovely with veg, poultry or a roast.

Chicory with chestnut purée *(endives sur purée de châtaignes)*

Prepare the purée as above and keep warm. Halve 4 heads of chicory lengthwise and braise in stock and a little butter for 20min. Grease a baking dish, add the purée and smooth out. Place the cooked leaves on top, dotted with butter. Grill for a few minutes, until the top is brown.

Chicken with chestnuts *(poulet aux châtaignes)*

Roast a chicken with sage and salt in a *covered* roasting pan. While it is cooking take some prepared chestnuts and simmer them in salted water with fennel leaves, celery, sage, a clove, and caraway seeds for 30 minutes, then strain. When the chicken is cooked, remove it and keep it warm. Put the chestnuts in the pan and roll them around gently in the chicken juices. Carve the chicken and serve with the juices and chestnuts from the pan.

Tourte de blettes

You'll see chard pie *(tourte de blettes)* for sale in Old Nice, for instance at René Socca. Surprisingly, this is a *sweet*, flavoured with lemon, sugar, dried raisins and pine nuts. Just look at the size of the chard on sale in France! This slice of the pie, from René's, was about the same size as this book!

Here's a 'ratatouille'-type recipe for this versatile vegetable. But what do you do with the leaves? You make a *tourte de blettes* — or a chard omelette (another popular dish), served with fresh shaved parmesan.

Chard stems Provence-style *(côtes de blettes à la provençale)*

Ingredients (for 4 people)

- 1 kg Swiss chard; this recipe uses the stems only, chopped (out of season, pac choy would be a good alternative)
- 1 onion, minced
- 500 g fresh tomatoes, deseeded and cut into small pieces
- 2 anchovy fillets
- 2 garlic cloves
- 1 tbsp olive oil
- sprig each of parsley and thyme, chopped
- salt and pepper

Sweat the onions in the olive oil. Add the tomatoes and let it all simmer for 15min over a very low heat. Then add salt, pepper and the thyme. Put in the anchovies and let them break up and melt.

Boil the chard stems for 10min. Add them to the onions and tomatoes. Let this simmer for 5min, then add the garlic and chopped parsley.

12

Turini! One of the first places we make for when we arrive at Nice. Surrounded by magnificent forests of firs and spruce, this eyrie is as silent and refreshing as a Christmas morning snowfall ... except when there's a motor rally on the famous hairpin road!

cime de l'arpiha

WALK

Distance: 9km/5.6mi; 2h40min

Grade: easy-moderate, with ascents/descents of about 280m/920ft; good tracks and paths. The scramble to the Arpiha summit demands some agility. Yellow PR waymarking. *IGN map 3741 ET*

Equipment: see page 9; sun protection (if only for sitting on the terrace at the Trois Vallées!)

Transport: 🚌 340 from Nice *(gare routière)* to Turini (09.00 Sun only; returns at 16.00); journey time 1h30min. Or 🚌 730 from Nice *(gare routière)* to Lantosque (08.00, 09.00 Mon-Sat); journey time 1h 05min, then by taxi to Turini (17km). *The taxi to/from Turini must be arranged in advance* (Lantosque taxi ☎ 04 93 03 04 68). Return on 🚌 730 at 17.36. Or 🚗 to the Col de Turini

Refreshments: cafés and restaurants at the Col de Turini

Points of interest:
Turini forest and pass
Authion Massif

Start out at the **Col de Turini**: walk north on the D68 (the road to the Authion, signposted 'Camp d'Argent'). After 700m/yds, at signpost 234 (**15min**), turn left. Follow this motorable track to the **Vacherie de Mantégas** and signpost 235. From July to September you can sample and buy local cheeses here.

From the dairy farm continue towards 'L'Arpiha' on a wide track signposted 'Itinéraire'. When you come to a **clearing** at spot height 1648 m (**30min**), signs point straight ahead to L'Arpiha. But instead, take the fork *half-left* here. This shady and mostly grassy path undulates along the south side of the Scoubayoun ridge. Breaks in the trees afford glimpses down left over Turini and the hairpin road. Keep right uphill at a fork 15 minutes along (as waymarked).

At signpost 236 (**1h05min**), go straight ahead for 'L'Arpiha'. You come to a second signpost numbered 236 at a grassy **col**. From here scramble up to the **Cime de l'Arpiha** (1634m/5360ft;

In the venerable forests of Turini, on the path to the Tête de Scoubayoun

1h25min), to enjoy magnificent views — west to the deeply-etched Planchette and Bollène valleys running towards the Vésubie, and east to the spread of the Authion.*

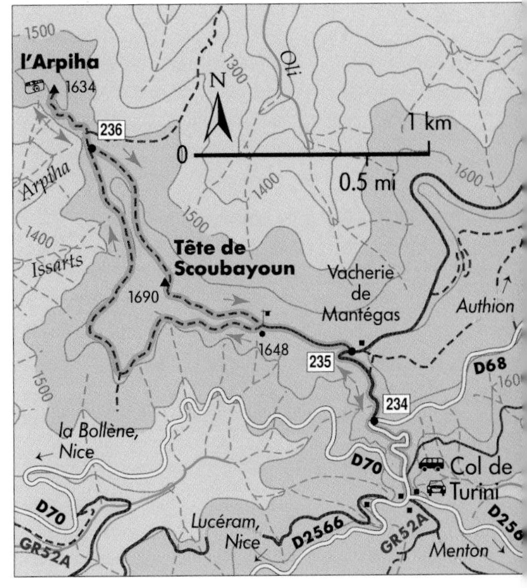

Return to the *first 236 signpost you met on the way up* and turn left. This path rises 150m/495ft in deep shade to the highest point in the walk, the **Tête de Scoubayoun**, then drops 50m/165ft back to the clearing at spot height 1648 m. Turn left here, to retrace your steps back to the **Col de Turini** (**2h40min**).

*A natural fortress because of its steep sides and strategic location on Italian border, the Authion has twice been the scene of bloody battles. Just after the birth of the French Republic, troops of the Austro-Sardinian coalition occupied the summit, and all Republican efforts to take it failed ... until Napoleon took charge. Encircling the mountain with troops, he cut off the enemy's supply lines and won the County of Nice for the Republicans. In World War II the Authion was the last place in France to be liberated, only two weeks before the end of the war, after heavy bombardment and a battle lasting three days. ***If you came by car, the circuit (signposted from the Col de Turini) round the Authion is a must!***

Les Trois Vallées

The Col de Turini comes alive with the Monte Carlo Rally in January (when it must be deafening), but in early spring and autumn, when the area is at its best for walking, all is silence.

The col is served by a cluster of hotels, but the oldest — and our favourite — is the Trois Vallées. Although we haven't stayed overnight for a few years, no trip to Nice is complete without afternoon tea on their terrace — especially in September, when the rowans are weighed down with fat red berries.

LES TROIS VALLEES
Col de Turini ✆ 04 93 04 23 23
open all year €-€€ (various 'menus')

standard four-course **regional menu** (25 €) always available:

entree: plate of mountain ham/salad with mountain ham/*sanguin* mushrooms (photo page 125)/crêpe filled with goats' cheese and minced mushrooms

mains: venison stew/trout stuffed with *foie gras* and apples in Normandy sauce/veal fillet with *girolles* (wild mushrooms)

interlude: samples of 'shepherds' specialities'

desserts: myrtle or raspberry tarte, mixed ice creams/*crème brûlée* with lavender

Naturally you'll find hearty mountain cooking at all the Turini hotels. With luck there will be wild boar or venison on the menu. We don't remember exactly how the Trois Vallées did the memorable dish of venison with mushrooms that we so enjoyed several years ago, but opposite is a rather unusual French recipe for fruited venison — a change from the more common sauce flavoured with red currants.

restaurants

VENISON STEAKS WITH BLACKBERRIES

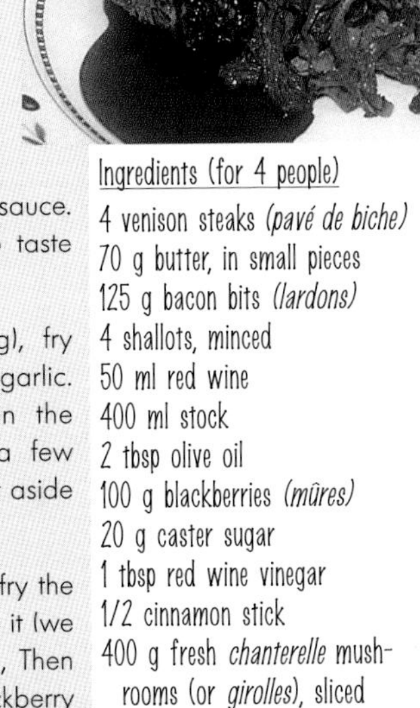

Gently cook the blackberries and sugar in a saucepan, stirring with a wooden spoon, until puréed. Add the vinegar, stock and cinnamon; bring to the boil, then simmer for 30min. Add the wine and cook for 5min more. Strain into another saucepan. Little by little, add 40 g of the butter, whisking all the time, and reduce until you have an fairly thick sauce. Season with salt and pepper to taste and keep warm.

In the rest of the butter (30 g), fry together the *lardons*, shallots and garlic. When they are golden, put in the mushrooms and cook for just a few minutes, then add the parsley. Set aside and keep warm.

In a heavy-bottomed frying pan, fry the venison in the olive oil as you like it (we think it's best a bit pink). Season, Then serve accompanied by the blackberry sauce and mushrooms. This recipe is ideal with potato cake (see page 60) — or even store-bought *rosti*.

Ingredients (for 4 people)

4 venison steaks *(pavé de biche)*
70 g butter, in small pieces
125 g bacon bits *(lardons)*
4 shallots, minced
50 ml red wine
400 ml stock
2 tbsp olive oil
100 g blackberries *(mûres)*
20 g caster sugar
1 tbsp red wine vinegar
1/2 cinnamon stick
400 g fresh *chanterelle* mushrooms (or *girolles*), sliced
2 cloves garlic, crushed
1 tbsp chopped parsley
salt and pepper to taste

We've been exploring the south of France for many years, doing what we like most — walking, eating and sampling local wines. Before we started our own publishing company and had more leisure (and money!), our excursions were often based on the many châteaux-hotels in the area. We toured from place to place, stayed a night or two, with a good hike during the day and a 5-star meal in the evening.

About ten years ago John started with the first of his food intolerances, when he was diagnosed coeliac (no more *baguettes* for the lunchtime picnic during a hike, no more *croissants* with 'elevenses', no more *tarte aux pommes*)!

Some coeliacs become lactose intolerant over time; many other people are lactose intolerant without being coeliac. True lactose intolerance doesn't just mean avoiding cow's milk, etc, but *all* milks, butters, creams, yoghurts, and cheeses — whether from cows, goats or sheep. Another blow — no more *fromage...*

Food intolerances are becoming ever more common, and we know *there are a lot of you out there!* Even if you have learned to cope at home, it can be very daunting to go on holiday. *Will the food in restaurants be safe? Will I be able to buy gluten- and dairy-free foods?*

If you suffer a food intolerance you have probably already learned at home that what initially seems a penance in fact becomes a challenge and eventually a joy. We eat far healthier meals now than we did before, with fewer additives.

EAT GF, DF

Nowhere is this more enjoyable than in the south of France, where olive oil, fish, tomatoes and 'alternative' grains and flours are basic to the diet. Many, many dishes are *naturally* gluten- and dairy-free.

Of course food intolerances *are* restrictive — in the sense that we have to carry, buy or bake gluten-free breads and sweets, and we always need access to dairy-free 'milk', 'cream', 'yoghurt' and 'butter'. So over the years we've sussed out eating gf, df around the Med, and it's *so simple.*

EATING IN RESTAURANTS

Many **entrées** are suitable, among them cold meat plates (like the one shown on page 56). Bring your own bread! Salads are also common, just avoid those with goats' cheese. The ubiquitous brown fish soup *(soupe de poissons;* also sold in supermarkets) is also gf, df — just bring your own croutons!

For **main courses** one is spoilt for choice. If you're a sauce addict, like John, here's some very good news. Sauces are virtually *always* made by 'reduction' (cooked over a moderate heat until it becomes syrupy, as opposed to being thickened with wheat flour). But of course, you will *ask in advance* (see inside back cover). Many **steaks** are served in a mushroom and wine sauce; at Le Pot d'Etain (see page 56) they are divine.

Anything '***à la provençale***' will be gf, df — generally this means with tomato, onion and garlic, as well as other spices and perhaps mushrooms, black olives and/or anchovies.

Fish dishes, unless grilled or poached, *may* well contain a least a dusting of flour, since fish is quite difficult to fry otherwise. *But not impossible.* If you ask, in a restaurant that *you trust*, they will do it without flour (or bring your own flour). Ask also if the sauce contains any cream or milk.

Give the **cheese course** a miss — unless, like John, you break out the 'lactase tablets' (now widely available at chemists and health food shops; just search the web) and treat yourself for a change. They really do work, and he uses them for special occasions (a magnificent cheese board) and even at the Caffé Promenade when we share a 'full works' omelette (it is so much better with cheese) or the *moules farcies* in butter.

We are usually too full to have **dessert**, but sometimes we share a slice of Michèle's chocolate cake (see page 61). Although made without flour, this does contain a bit of butter. Other restaurants have chocolate sweets that are completely gf, df.

And as you may know already, *socca*, Nice's speciality snack, which makes a smashing lunch, is 100% gf, df.

SELF-CATERING

While many hotels cater for food intolerances, we discovered the joy of self-catering — whether in a country cottage or an apart-hotel in the city — years ago. What a liberation! Room to swing a cat (or, more likely, chop up a rabbit). Tables where you can spread out your maps and bus timetables. Sofas to loll about on with a good book on a rainy day.

But for a special occasion, we might just book a night or two in one of the châteaux for old time's sake; it's relatively easy to cope for just a couple of nights. Then back to base with the laundry and gf bread waiting in the freezer.

Gf, df shopping

After getting all the staples (and the other goodies mentioned at the right) from the supermarket and fresh produce from the market, our next port of call will be the health food shop, to collect all the gf, df things we'll need for the whole stay. This chain is called **Au Bio Marché**, and the main branch in the centre of the city is at 2 Rue de la Buffa (just west of Place Grimaldi; 33 on the plan; ☎ 04 93 82 56 14).

Usually we can get everything we want here, but there is a much larger branch just a short way out of the centre, on the 14 bus route to Mont Boron (Walk 1). Watch the names of the stops as the bus climbs the hill: pass Terra Amata and A de Joly; get off at the *next* stop, Pré Fossati. Then walk a short way downhill, and the shop (10 Corniche André de Joly, ☎ 04 93 26 38 02)

GF, DF supermarket shopping

Our favourite supermarket chain, Casino, stocks some very useful products (but not in their mini-markets):

Tournolive is top of the list — a dairy-free cooking/baking/spreading margarine, which tastes delicious and does *not* spit when used for frying, as it contains 60% sunflower oil;

soya milk and yoghurts — natural or flavoured — which can be bought in small containers;

Camargue salt *(fleur de sel)*; the brand sold in Casino comes in such a lovely container with cork lid that it makes a great and inexpensive gift for those back home;

jams (Baptistin Feraud is particularly good;

gf, df tinned 'stews': Casino's own-brand *Saucisses aux lentilles à la graisse d'oil* or *Petit salé aux lentilles.* Mix either with a tin of chopped tomatoes and a glass of wine and *voilà*: dinner in a moment! (*Beware*: most other brands of these tinned stews are *not* gf, so read the label)

soupe de poissons à la provençale: this comes in a large glass jar and all those we have seen are gf, df.

will be on your left, in a small shopping area. (There is also a large car park, if you are driving). A third shop is well west of the centre at 212 Avenue Californie (✆ 04 93 71 52 88), but we've not been there.

Some of the things to look out for at Au Bio Marché are:

- simply delicious soya yoghurts. There is a great variety available in small sizes (150 g), in both glass jars and plastic containers;
- soya or rice 'milks', such as Provamel Bio Soya;
- soya 'cream' — a *must* for cooking. In France it is called Provamel Soya *Cuisine* (it's the same product that is available in the UK as Provamel Soya *Dream*);
- gluten-free breads: try not only the widely-available Italian brands like Schär and Glutano, but look out too for the 'sliced country bread' made by the French company Pleniday (now also available in the UK); it is perfect with the *bourride* recipe on page 68;
- gluten-free biscuits: Schär has both sweet and plain, and their biscuits for cheese are superb;
- gluten-free flour: all kinds of flours are on sale — why not get some chick-pea flour to make *socca* at home (see recipe on page 30)?
- Rapunzel 'Soma' dairy-free margarine made in Avignon; contains 60% sunflower oil and *doesn't spit* when frying.

Gf, df cooking

We've made all the **recipes** in this book using gluten- and dairy-free ingredients. Basically we just used a 1:1 substitution —

Gf, df dinner at Le Pot d'Etain – a mixed salad to start and *boeuf à la bourguignonne*

remember, we are just amateur cooks — and the cooking method was unchanged. We've been more than happy with the results! The

only cooking problem we have is with *frying,* when the recipe calls for a mixture of oil and butter (or just butter). Most vegetable fats spit all over the place. But Tournolive (from supermarkets) and Soma (from health food shops) are far better than any other 100% df spreads we've used because they contain *less water.*

CONVERSION TABLES

Weights

10 g	1/2 oz
25 g	1 oz
50 g	2 oz
110 g	4 oz
200 g	7 oz
350 g	12 oz
450 g	1 lb
700 g	1 lb 8 oz
900 g	2 lb
1.35 g	3 lb

Volume

15 ml	1 tbsp
55 ml	2 fl oz
75 ml	3 flz oz
150 ml	1/4 pt
275 ml	1/2 pt
570 ml	1 pt
1 l	1-3/4 pt
1.5 l	2-1/2 pt

Oven temperatures

°C	°F	gas mark
140°C	275°F	1
150°C	300°F	2
170°C	325°F	3
180°C	350°F	4
190°C	375°F	5
200°C	400°F	6
220°C	425°F	7
230°C	430°F	8
240°C	475°F	9

MENU ITEMS

à point medium rare
agneau lamb
de lait milk-fed
agnelet young lamb
aïado lamb with herbs and garlic
aigre-doux sweet and sour
ail garlic
aïoli mayonnaise with garlic (see p. 68-69)
aligot potato purée with cream, butter, garlic and fresh cheese
aiglefin haddock
allumette puff pastry
amande almond
amer bitter
anchoïade sauce of anchovies, olive oil and garlic
anchois anchovy
andouille smoked tripe sausage
andouillette small tripe sausage
aneth dill
anis aniseed
arachide peanut
arête fish bone *(sans arêtes* = filleted)
aromates aromatic spices
artichaut artichoke
asperges asparagus
assiette de plate of
avocat avocado
basilic basil
beignet fritter
bleu very rare
biche female deer
blettes Swiss chard
boeuf beef
bourride fish stew; see p. 68
brandade de morue salt cod
brochette skewered
cabillaud salt cod fritters
caille quail
caillette pork and vegetable faggot
calamars squid
canard duck
caneton duckling
carré cutlet or chop from best end of neck
carvi caraway
celéri celery
celéri-rave celeriac
cèpes ceps (delicate, highly-prized mushrooms)
champignons mushrooms
de paris button —
chanterelles golden-coloured mushrooms
chevreau kid
chevreuil roe-deer
choix, au choice of
chou cabbage
chou-fleur cauliflower
confit preserved
coquillages shellfish
coquilles st-jacques scallops
côte chop, side
coulis thick sauce
courge pumpkin
crabe crab
crevettes
grises shrimp
roses prawns
crudités raw vegetables
daube stew; see p. 102
daurade/dorade sea-bream
dinde young hen turkey
dindon turkey
écrevisses freshwater crayfish
entrecôte rib steak
escabêche marinated fish or poultry, served cold
escargots snails
estouffade beef stew with onions, herbs and red wine
faisan pheasant
foie gras goose liver
fricandeau slice of topside veal
fritures tiny fried fish
fruits de mer seafood
gambas giant prawns
gibier game
gratiné browned with butter and breadcrumbs
grenadin thick veal escalope
grenouille frog
cuisse de — frogs' legs
grillé grilled
farci stuffed
fleurs de courgettes courgette flowers
haricots beans
— *verts* green beans
homard lobster
huîtres oysters
jambon ham
fumé smoked

GLOSSARY

langouste spiny lobster
langue tongue
lapereau young rabbit
lapin rabbit
légumes vegetables
lièvre hare
civet de — jugged hare
longue loin
lotte (de mer) monkfish
loup (de mer) sea-bass
miel honey
mignon small (round) piece
morue cod
moules mussels
noix nuts
oignon onion
pain/pan bread
bagnat thick sandwich; see p. 28
pâtes pasta
pané with breadcrumbs
panisses chick-pea fritters
persil parsley
persillade chopped parsley and garlic
petit small
pignons pine nuts
pissaladière pizza; see p. 28
pistou mixture of garlic, basil, tomatoes and olive oil, blended with mortar and pestle
poire pear
poireau leek
poisson fish
poivron sweet pepper
potage thick soup
poussin baby chicken
Provençale, à la with tomatoes, olive oil, garlic
raisins grapes
rascasse scorpion fish
ravigote sauce with onions, herbs, mushrooms, wine vinegar
rémoulade sauce with mayonnaise, mustard, capers, anchovies, herbs
rognons kidneys
rouget red mullet
rouille mayonnaise-like sauce with peppers, garlic and saffron
safran saffron
salade Niçoise salad with tuna, tomatoes, anchovies, hard-boiled egg, black olives
sanglier wild boar
sarriette savoury, bitter herb
socca 'pancake' made with chick-pea flour; see p. 28
saumon salmon
sole sole
suprême boneless breast
tapenade paste of black olives, anchovies and capers (called 'Provençal caviar')
tarte open pastry case
telline small clam
terrine cold 'loaf' of fish, meat or pâté (named for the container in which it is cooked)
tourte sweet-filled pastry case, pie
de blettes chard pie (see p. 127)
truccha Nice-style omelette with Swiss chard or wild asparagus and garlic
truite trout
turbot/turbotin turbot
velouté white sauce
veau veal
volaille poultry

SHOPPING TERMS

anchovies *anchois*
apple *pomme*
artichoke *artichaut*
asparagus *asperges*
avocado *avocat*
bacon bits *(lardons)*
unsmoked *(lardons nature)*
bass, sea *loup de mer*
bay leaf *laurier*
beans *haricots*
green *haricots verts*
beef *boeuf*
cuts:
boneless *sans os*
fillet *filet*
flank *bavette*
fore rib *entrecôte*
rib *côte*
rump *rumsteak*
shin *jarret*
shoulder *paleron*
sirloin *contrefilet*
strip loin *faux-filet*
tongue *langue*
beer *bière*
blackberries *mûres*
brandy *cognac*
bread *pain*
bream, sea *daurade*
butter *beurre*
cake *gâteau*
caraway *carvi*
carrot *carotte*
celeriac *celéri-rave*
celery *céleri*
chard, Swiss *blettes*
cheese *fromage*
cherries *cerises*
chestnuts, sweet *châtaignes*
chicken *poulet*
baby *poussin*
chocolate *chocolat*

cider *cidre*
cloves *girofles*
cod *morue*
coffee *café*
condiments *condiments*
corn
 meal *farine de maïs*
 starch *amidon de maïs*
courgettes *courgettes*
crab *crabe*
crayfish *écrevisses*
cream *crème*
cucumber *concombre*
duck *canard*
 preserved *confit*
eggs *oeufs*
fennel *fenouil*
fish *poisson*
flour (wheat) *farine*
 chick-pea *farine de pois chiches*
 corn *farine de maïs*
fruit *fruit*
game *gibier*
garlic *ail*
goose *oie*
 grease *graisse d'oie*
 liver *foie gras*
grapes *raisins*
haddock *aiglefin*
ham *jambon*
 smoked *fumé*
hare *lièvre*
herbs *herbes*
ice cream *glace*
juice *jus*
juniper *genièvre*
lamb *agneau*
milk-fed *agneau de lait*
 cuts:
 boneless *sans os*
 cutlets from best end of neck *carré*
 leg (including chump) *gigot*
 loin *filet*
 shouler *épaule*
leek *poireau*
lemon *citron*
lettuce *laitue*
liver *foie*
lobster *homard*
 spiny *langouste*
milk *lait*
monkfish *lotte de mer*
mullet, red *rouget*
mushrooms *champignons*
mussels *moules*
mustard *moutarde*
nuts *noix*
 peanuts *arachides*
olive oil *huile d'olive*
onions *oignons*
oysters *huîtres*
parsley *persil*
pasta *pâtes*
pastry *pâtisserie*
pear *poire*
peas *pois/petits pois*
pepper (spice) *poivre*
pepper (sweet) *poivron*
pheasant *faisan*
pine nuts *pignons*
pork *porc*
 rind *couennes*
 cuts:
 boneless *sans os*
 chop *côte*
 cutlet from best end of neck *carré*
 escalope *escalope*
 fillet *filet*
 loin *longue*
potatoes *pommes de terre*
poultry *volaille*
prawns *crevettes*
 giant *gambas*
pumpkin *courge*
quail *caille*
rabbit *lapin*
 young *lapereau*
raspberries *framboises*
rice *riz*
rosemary *romarin*
saffron *safran*
salmon *saumon*
salt *sel*
 sea *(fleur de sel)*
sausage
 fresh *saucisse*
 dry *saucisson*
scallops *coquilles (St-Jacques)*
scorpion fish *rascasse*
shallots *echalotes*
shellfish *coquillages*
shrimp *crevettes grises*
snails *escargots*
sole *sole*
soup *soupe*
soya *soja*
spices *épices*
spinach *épinards*
sugar *sucre*
tarragon *estragon*
tea *thé*
thyme *thym*
tomatoes *tomates*
trout *truite*
tuna *thun*
turbot *turbot, turbotin*
turkey *dindon*
 young *dinde*
veal *veau*
 cuts:
 boneless *sans os*
 chop *côte*
 fillet *filet*
 kidneys *rognons*
 liver *foie*
 loin *carré*
 shin, knuckle *jarret*
 shoulder *épaule*
 sweetbreads *ris*
 topside *noix*
vegetables *légumes*
venison steaks *pavé de biche*
vinegar *vinagre*
 wine *de vin*
water *eau*
 still *sans gaz*
 sparkling *avec gaz*
watercress *cresson*
wine *vin*
 dry *sec*
 red *rouge*
 white *blanc*

bold type: photograph; *italic type:* map

INDEX

Second edition
Published by Sunflower Books
PO Box 36061, London SW7 3WS
www.sunflowerbooks.co.uk

ISBN 978-1-85691-338-6

Cover photograph: Nice marina, with Notre-Dame du Port in the background (Walk 1)

Photographs and maps: John Underwood
Cookery editor: Marina Bayliss
Series designed by Jocelyn Lucas
A CIP catalogue record for this book is available from the British Library.
Printed and bound in China by WKT Company Ltd

Before you go ...
log on to
www.sunflowerbooks.co.uk
and click on '**updates**', to see if we have been notified of any changes to the routes or restaurants.

When you return ...
do let us know if any routes have changed because of road-building, storm damage or the like. Have any of our restaurants closed — or any new ones opened *on the route of the walk?* (Not Nice restaurants, please; these books are not intended to be complete restaurant guides!)

Send your comments to mail@sunflowerbooks.co.uk